D0627800

DRIVING THE DRUNK OFF THE ROAD

DRIVING THE DRUNK OFF THE ROAD

A Handbook For Action

SANDY GOLDEN

QUINCE
MILL
BOOKS

OLD WESTBURY LIBRARY

Dedication

This book is dedicated to my mother, Adele Wolman. For three years she has supported my family so that I could work on the drunk-driving issue and take the time necessary to compile my findings. Without her this book would not have been possible, nor would the anti-drunk driving movement be as far along as it is.

OLD WESTBURY LIBRARY

HE 5620

.D7 G64

copy 1

All rights reserved. No part of this book may be used or reproduced in any manner whatsoever without written permission except in the case of brief quotations embodied in critical articles and reviews. Permission is given to copy the sample petitions and letters.

Copyright © 1983 by Sandy Golden

Published by Quince Mill Books
               21 Quince Mill Court
               Gaithersburg, Maryland 20878

First Printing

Cover design by Sally Counihan.

Library of Congress Cataloging in Publication Data

Golden, Sandy, 1945-
     Driving the drunk off the road.

     Includes index.
     1. Drinking and traffic accidents—Government policy—United States—Citizen participation—Handbooks, manuals, etc.   2. Drunk driving—Government policy—United States—Citizen participation—Handbooks, manuals, etc.   I. Title.
HE5620.D7G64   1983   363.1'257'0973   83-8982

ISBN 0-914757-01-6 (paperback)
ISBN 0-914757-00-8 (hardcover)

Manufactured in the United States of America

ACKNOWLEDGEMENTS

This book reflects the efforts of many people, most of whom volunteered their time and resources, and to all of whom I feel deeply indebted.

Dr. Jim Nichols of the National Highway Traffic Safety Administration (NHTSA) deserves special thanks for conceiving the idea for the first book I wrote on this issue and for continuing to encourage me to work on the drunk-driving problem. This book is an outgrowth of my first one, and if I have a mentor for my work, it is Dr. Nichols. Other staffers at NHTSA also deserve credit, but there are too many to name.

Two distinquished retired newsmen, Roger Farquhar, and Lawrence McDaniel in particular, gave my manuscript meticulous readings and solid, professional advice which helped turn it into a readable book. The Washington law firm of Onek, Kline and Farr took the book on as a *pro-bono* project: my warm thanks to Joseph Onek, who was Deputy Counsel to President Carter and specializes in health issues, for reviewing the book for libel and for suggesting improvements.

I am especially grateful to Dr. Leonard Kapiloff, publisher of the Sentinel Newspapers and president of Comprint, Inc. who donated the typesetting and related pre-press services. The skilled help unstintingly given by many of the people at Comprint was invaluable: editor Jim Streit, production manager Raya Koren, typographer Cindy Hammett, art director Sally Counihan, and especially data processing manager Ned Lynch. "To help save lives" he gave up evenings and weekends for two months to get the book into type.

Joe Matera taught me how to use my home computer, which greatly simplified my work. My good neighbor Renee Pindell helped proofread the manuscript. Neal Potter, a member of the Montgomery County Council, gave me his time and help on this project.

There are many other people—victims, police, students, teachers, religious leaders, citizen activists—an endless list of them who for reasons of space must be unnamed. But to all of them, I sincerely say thank you.

My daughter Karen, who is sixteen years old, made many contributions and sacrifices to help get this project completed. My son, Jason (4), also helped greatly in his own way. Words are not sufficient to describe the deep appreciation, thanks, and love that I have for the never-ending support, encouragement and faith my special friend and spouse of 17 years, Sylvia, has contributed to this book. May it save many lives.

CONTENTS

Contents

PREFACE

Our son, Tommie, was 15 years old when he was killed by a drunk driver. Shortly after Tommie's death in July 1980, our outrage over what had happened to him became overwhelming. We learned he—and we—were victims of this country's most frequently committed violent crime, drinking and driving, and that something had to be done to prevent future tragedies. But we didn't know what to do. At about this time, we met Sandy Golden. He gave us the strategies that turned our anger and grief into positive action.

Sandy Golden is a highly skilled, award winning journalist and is one of the most effective investigative reporters in the nation. In May 1980, he was an off-camera reporter for WDVM, the CBS television station in Washington D.C. At that time, he helped put together a news series about a five-month-old baby girl, Laura Lamb, who was permanently paralyzed from her neck down by a repeat offender drunk driver. What had happened to that child was outrageous and inexcusable. Drunk-driving laws in Maryland were among the weakest in the United States. Enforcement stunk. The news series had immediate impact and triggered massive drunk-driving reform in Maryland. The story was so compelling that the Governor could not ignore it.

After doing that story, Sandy quickly learned that drunk driving was a monstrous national tragedy that was being neglected by virtually all levels of government, the public and the media. Large numbers of innocent people of all ages were being slaughtered on our highways and little or nothing was being done to correct the problem. There was a plague of anguish across our land and the experts were predicting that it was going to get much worse. Sandy did not ignore the situation. He believed that the issue deserved the full-time efforts of an unbridled investigative reporter, whose only loyalty would be to the truth. Reform in Maryland was underway, so he left his television job in an effort to bring the issue to the American public and to get something done about it. He has been laboring on the issue now for three years, and has become without a doubt the most knowledgeable journalist in the United States on the subject of drunk driving and is one of the most effective strategists in the history of the issue.

In August 1980, he became the first executive director (unsalaried) of Mothers Against Drunk Drivers (MADD). He helped to get the organization off the ground, and promoted the concept of citizen activist groups to combat the problem. After leaving MADD, he donated his time to numerous victim activist groups and taught them what they needed to know. He helped generate unprecedented media attention to the problem. The Maryland Chapter of MADD was one of the prime beneficiaries of his teachings.

He has interviewed more than a thousand people connected with the issue and travelled to more than 26 states speaking out on the problem and calling for reform. Many people started listening to his advice and the issue has now been turned on its ear. He developed several very effective strategies, including the concept of a task force in every community to work for a reduction of death and injury that stems from alcohol-related crashes.

We know for a fact that his advice is sound and that his methods work. Eight counties in Maryland have appointed local task forces and the results of these task forces have been lifesaving. He is directly responsible for the establishment of numerous other state and local task forces (in California, Pennsylvania, West Virginia, Virginia and Missouri to name a few). In Missouri, the RID (Remove Intoxicated Drivers) chapter in St. Louis County followed his advice and led the way to a three-decade low in alcohol-related fatalities in their state.

Sandy was the first national leader to be recognized for his work on the issue and was given a national public service award for his "extraordinary contribution to the cause of highway safety" by the National Highway Traffic Safety Administration (NHTSA). He has also written a manual for NHTSA that teaches the public how to organize to save lives and reduce injuries.

He conceived the idea for the Presidential Commission on Drunk Driving and fought to make it a reality. He authored a letter to President Reagan calling for the creation of the Commission and helped lobby the letter through Congress until a majority of Congress, both House and Senate, signed it and it was hand-delivered to the President by Congressman James Hansen of Utah. He also authored the petition used by MADD that called for the Commission.

Sandy knows what he is talking about when it comes to drunk driving. Maryland MADD has used many of the strategies outlined in this book. We have been able to achieve an unprecedented reduction in drunk-driving fatalities. By 1982, alcohol-related auto fatalities in Maryland

decreased 27 percent below the 1981 level—an 18-year low
(non-alcohol related auto fatalities for this period dropped
only three percent). By 1983, alcohol-related traffic deaths
decreased 71 percent in our county.

We listened to Sandy Golden and now ask that you read
what he has to say. His message is simple. Although it
appears that much progress has been made during the past
three years to rid our roads of drunk drivers, the fact is that
the surface has hardly been scratched. The lives saved to
date are only a small fraction of the number that should
have been saved.

This book clearly shows how concerned citizens and
students can get involved and help make their communities
safer places to live. *Driving The Drunk Off The Road* goes
far beyond his previous work on the issue and is designed to
once and for all bring under control the leading cause of
death of young people in our country. If you have already
started an anti-drunk driving group or want to start one, you
need to know what he has to say. If you are concerned about
drunk driving and the threat drunk drivers pose to yourself
and family, you need to read this book. It tells the truth.
And that is what you need to know, because your life and
the lives of your children are at stake.

Tom and Dot Sexton

Publisher's Note: Tom and Dot Sexton are co-leaders of
Maryland MADD (Mothers Against Drunk Drivers), one of
the most effective anti-drunk driving groups in the country.
Tom Sexton is also a member of the Maryland State Task
Force on Drunk Driving. The Sextons' successful efforts
have been recognized and given national prominence by
reporting on television (on such shows as *ABC's 20/20*) and
the local and national press.

A FOREWORD
TO YOUNG PEOPLE

The most precious gifts we all have in common are our lives and our health. Teen-agers, though the change from childhood to adulthood is often emotionally painful and frustrating, have promising futures as long as they enjoy good health.

Living a full lifespan can be a beautiful experience beyond imagination. You have to live a full life to appreciate it. Everyone wants to live and be healthy. No one wants to lose his life before he has had a chance to really live. And no one has a right to take a life or jeopardize a person's health. But there are irresponsible people in every community who routinely kill and seriously injure teen-agers and get away with it.

The victims suffer a brutal fate. What happens to those kids, so full of life, is horrible, nightmarish. And it can happen to you. If you want to live and keep your health, this may be the most important book you will read as a student. Reading it **could** save your life.

This book will show you how to protect yourself and your family and friends. It contains up-to-date information. Much of the material is new. Your life is on the line. Your future is at stake. If you fail to take the time to read this book, you could ruin your chance at life.

You need to know that there is a very serious and uncontrolled health and safety epidemic in your community called drunk driving. And to be quite blunt about it, you don't know enough about the problem. The terrible and harsh reality is that **your life is in imminent danger from drunk drivers.** Everyone is at risk. It is a very real and frightening problem that you need to take the time to learn the full truth about, so you can understand and assess how much of a risk you face and how you can take steps to lessen your chances of being seriously hurt or even fatally injured.

Ignoring the problem is like playing Russian roulette. Unless you take steps to protect yourself and unless corrective action is taken in every state and community in the nation, sooner or later one of every two people in this country is going to be involved in an alcohol-related crash in his lifetime. One of them could be you.

The fact is that without any warning, within seconds, you could be killed or seriously injured while on the way home from school today. It could happen to you at any time on any given day. And as unfair as it may seem, it could happen through no fault of your own. But you will be just as dead or just as crippled or just as disfigured, even though you were totally innocent and minding your own business. A simple trip to a store could be your last. A similar fate could befall a member of your family or any of your friends.

Use your imagination and visualize what life would be like if you were confined to a bed or wheelchair because a drunk driver paralyzed you from the neck down and you could never use your arms or legs again. And consider the effect on your life if one of your parents (or both) or a close friend was killed by an irresponsible person who had too much to drink to be able to drive safely. It's not pleasant even to think about, but it happens to young people like you every day in communities in every state in the nation. The frightening truth is that **you** could be the next victim.

However, you can substantially improve your chances of not becoming involved in an alcohol-related crash by taking the time to read and understand the material in this book. You should be acutely aware of the seriousness of the problem and the threat it poses to your life. You have the right to know the truth about a problem that has become a major cause of sudden, violent death and serious injuries which often leave young people crippled for life or severely disfigured or physically impaired. You also have a right to know what can be done about the problem and why not enough **is** being done. This book will give you that information.

It is written in the hope that if enough students, parents and teachers read it, fewer young people will be killed or crippled for life as a result of what has become the most frequently committed, and most neglected, violent crime in America—drunk driving.

carefully or were passengers in vehicles being operated by responsible drivers.

In May 1980 on a Saturday afternoon, for example, 13-year-old Cari Lightner was walking along a bicycle lane on her way to a church carnival in Fair Oaks, California, when a car suddenly swerved off the road and hit her from behind. Cari was thrown 120 feet to her death. The driver did not even stop to render first aid; Cari was left to die by the side of the road.

The man who "murdered" Cari was a repeat offender drunk driver who had been arrested three times before. When he struck and killed Cari, he had been out of jail on bail for only two days for yet another hit-and-run drunk-driving collision.

Shortly before Cari's tragic death, on the other side of the nation, 15-year-old Tommie Sexton Jr. was returning to his home in Bowie, Maryland, from a fishing trip in a neighbor's car when he too was killed by a drunk driver.

What happened to Cari and Tommie happens all too frequently to innocent teen-agers. They are but two of the 25,000 young people who have been killed by drunk drivers in the past five years.

But teen-agers themselves are often at fault in drunk-driving collisions. According to NHTSA statistics, some 60 percent of fatally-injured young drivers were found to have alcohol in their blood prior to the collision and 43 percent had legally-intoxicating levels. Although teen-agers comprise just eight percent of the licensed driver population in the United States and account for only six percent of the vehicle miles travelled, 15 percent of all drunk drivers who are involved in a collision are under 21 years of age.

Why has this been allowed to happen? Why are you, sometimes through no fault of your own, in danger of losing your life or being seriously injured by a drunk driver?

3

The answers are simple. Until recently (about the time Cari Lightner was killed), all levels of government had failed to take the steps necessary to protect your life. And it is those failures at the federal, state and local levels that have put your life in jeopardy. The cumulative toll of life taken by drunk drivers has become a monstrous national disgrace. Some people say it is "America's greatest tragedy."

But as grim as the statistics and the realities of the situation are, there is hope. There are steps you can take to protect your life and substantially increase your chances of survival. There are also moves you can make individually and collectively to make your state and community safer places to live.

First, it is necessary to understand the general nature of the drunk-driving issue so you can protect yourself intelligently and work for effective reform of the drunk-driving problem.

THE UNVARNISHED TRUTH

Currently, drunk driving is the most frequently committed and most neglected violent crime in the nation. Drunk drivers are literally getting away with murder. This is because there is an uncontrolled epidemic of dangerous alcohol-impaired drivers in practically every community and not enough is being done by public officials to protect the public's safety.

There are so many drunk drivers on the roads at all hours of the day and night, seven days a week, that **your streets are not safe**. Weekend nights, the most popular dating times for teen-agers (between the hours of 10 p.m. and 3 a.m.), are the most dangerous. Anytime you or a member of your family leave home, even on a routine trip to the grocery, a drunk driver, without any warning, could

The Commission to date has been ineffective and slow to move.

On Capitol Hill, Senator Claiborne Pell of Rhode Island and Maryland Congressman Michael Barnes spearheaded the passage of a new federal law that suggests guidelines for states to follow. Senator Pell became interested in the issue when two of his staffers were killed in Maryland in separate collisions caused by drunk drivers in an 18-month period. Congressman Barnes, moved by the Laura Lamb tragedy in his state, responded to a request of a reporter to get involved.

But taking into account everything the federal government is now doing to protect the public from drunk drivers (and there are many who say it still is not doing enough), drunk driving must be combatted primarily at the state and local levels if alcohol-related death and injuries are to be significantly reduced.

The drunk-driving problem exists locally because in **every** state, the laws that deal with it often are inadequate, poorly enforced, and not well adjudicated. Also, state administrative policy and procedures dealing with drunk drivers are loaded with dangerous deficiencies.

Task forces have been set up to deal with the problem in 39 states in just the past three years. But despite this, it remains largely uncontrolled and not adequately dealt with. There is much that needs to be done in every state; the surface has hardly been scratched.

At the county and city levels, there is a "system" that is supposed to protect the public from drunk drivers. It is made up of police, prosecutors, judges, probation officers, rehabilitation counselors and others. But in every such jurisdiction, with few exceptions, the local system is dangerously flawed and inadequate. The deficiencies include lax enforcement, prosecution and adjudication, and such problems as businesses that routinely sell beer to minors. In the schools, programs designed to call attention to the dangers of drinking and driving are often poorly put together and out of date. Programs to curtail teen drinking and driving simply do not exist in far too many schools.

Such flaws at the local level are the chief reason people are continually killed and injured by drunk drivers. If progress is ever to be made, these problems must be identified and corrected.

But the drunk-driving crisis is more than a series of systems throughout the nation that are flawed and inadequate. In the final analysis, it is primarily a **political problem.** Bringing it under control does not require new technology. We have the knowledge to correct the situation substantially and save many lives, but such knowledge is simply not being used. We know what needs to be done. But the elected and appointed officials have not and will not take the necessary steps to effect a solution. It is up to the public to pressure officials to get reform. Since teenagers all too often are the victims of drunk drivers, it is necessary for them to **demand** that everything possible be done to protect their lives. This is necessary because society, which is controlled by adults, cannot be trusted to correct the problem and has let teen-agers down to the point where alcohol-related crashes are the leading cause of death for young people. "Teen power" can change that. It's up to you.

NOTES

1. The word accident is purposefully not used in this book because there is no such thing as a drunk-driving "accident." Such an event is a crash or collision that follows the crime of drinking to excess and driving at the same time. When someone is injured or killed by a drunk driver, they are the victim of a violent crime. **They are not accident victims.**

2

WHAT CAN BE DONE
ABOUT DRUNK DRIVERS?

There is no complete solution to the drunk-driving problem. And one may never exist. Just as it is impossible to eliminate the crime of bank robbery, it is impossible to get all drunk drivers off the highways. Drunk driving is an ill that society will always have to contend with and strive to keep under control.

Unfortunately, over the past decade, the problem has been neglected at all levels of government and is now out of control. There is, however, information available that will allow any governmental agency to devise effective strategies to protect the public and save lives. If the problem is properly managed by federal, state and local governments, alcohol-related death and injuries in every state and community in the nation can be significantly lowered.

Instead of a yearly death toll of 25,000 killed and 650,000 injured, at least half that number could be spared.[1]

It is also absolutely possible for local governments, even if state and federal agencies totally ignore the problem, to take immediate, simple steps that will dramatically lessen the odds against people being killed or injured by drunk drivers.

THIS IS WHAT SHOULD BE DONE

The highest elected official of each county and major city should adopt the position, honestly and firmly, that drunk driving will no longer be tolerated in that particular jurisdiction.

The official then needs to set up a task force of **qualified** individuals to assess, accurately and completely, the system that is supposed to protect the public from drunk drivers and to devise a strategy to bring the problem under control. The investigation must uncover and document every life-threatening flaw and deficiency in the system and, based on already known methods and techniques, recommend how to overcome the problems uncovered. If the task force performs competently and its recommendations are implemented, the goal of saving lives and reducing injuries will be achieved.

In every community where drunk driving is out of control, arrests must increase. Well-thought-out, continuous, publicity and education campaigns must be launched to change attitudes about drinking and driving. The increased numbers of those arrested must be effectively prosecuted and the courts must correctly punish and mete out appropriate education and treatment to convicted drunk drivers.

Merchants who, because of lax or non-existent law enforcement, routinely sell alcoholic beverages to minors or intoxicated persons, must be caught and prosecuted. They must be made to understand that their illegal behavior is unconscionable and will no longer be tolerated.

The local school system must take an honest look at alcohol education and traffic safety programs and institute changes where appropriate. School officials must recognize their responsibility in the effort to decrease the teen death rate and nurture anti-drunk driving student groups and help them gather public support to bring the problem under control.

Concerned citizens must work together to obtain effective reform so their communities will be safer places. Victim activist groups like MADD and RID should be organized in every community to demand, along with the student groups, that elected officials promptly take all necessary steps to bring and keep the problem under control.

Student groups must use peer pressure to help prevent alcohol abuse among teen-agers. If there is no effective victim activist group in the community, the student group can work alone to demand significant corrective action until it becomes a reality.

Legislative leaders must take the time to learn the dynamics of the alcohol-crash problem and lead the efforts to enact tough new laws. While more than two dozen states have approved new drunk-driving legislation in the past three years, not one has enacted all the laws necessary to provide maximum public protection.

A governor's task force in each state should be formed to develop a comprehensive **master plan** indicating what the state needs to do to coordinate activities necessary to control drunk drivers.

The state task force must take a **total systems approach** and investigate the state police function, the prosecutorial function, the role of the courts and probation departments, and the driver licensing, education and state health departments. Every component and aspect of the state's drunk driving control system has to be scrutinized.

In addition, the role of each state in alcohol beverage control must be evaluated, as well as the current tax structure on alcoholic beverages. Funds to finance needed drunk driver control at the state and local level must also be developed. (This can be accomplished without putting any extra burden on the non-drinking/driving public.)

The Governor, working with the state legislature, must provide the leadership to get corrective legislation enacted quickly. And he must work to implement other findings of the task force, provided its work is competently done. If a state already has a task force, its efforts should be reviewed to assure it is going about its lifesaving business in the most effective manner possible.

Victim and student activist groups must be alert to make sure that state officials do everything possible to protect the public from drunk drivers.

At the federal level, Congress must come to grips with the problem of how to help state and local governments pay for the cost of bringing the problem under control.

Although Congress recently passed "guideline" legislation that will provide extra funds for states that meet the necessary criteria to attack the problem, the "extra" funds are but a fraction of the money needed. And with the estimated cost of drunk-driving damage pegged at more than $24 billion a year, the $125 million made available by Congress will hardly cause a dent in the overall problem.

What Congress needs to do is take a hard look at what has become a **"sacred cow"** in this country — the federal tax structure on alcohol. Federal excise taxes on alcohol have not been increased since 1951. This is because the beverage alcohol industry has one of the most powerful and best-organized lobbying groups in Washington. The alcohol industry has been able to influence Congress so effectively that for the past 30 years the taxes on its products have been kept frozen. It is clearly not paying its fair share for the damage to society that its products cause.

Industry leaders argue that their taxes are high enough.

Groups like the Center for Science in the Public Interest (CSPI) contend the alcohol beverage industry and alcohol consumers should pay more for programs needed as a result of alcohol abuse. Because excise taxes have not been raised for the past 30 years, the CSPI says, the price of alcoholic beverages has decreased in relation to other consumer products so that alcoholic beverage consumers and producers are now being subsidized, in effect, by the taxpayers. "Some beer is now cheaper than soda," notes George Hacker, associate director for alcohol policies at the CSPI.

If the alcohol taxes had been adjusted to keep pace with inflation since 1951, the government would receive an additional $14 billion in revenues each year. And if the tax on beer and wine were adjusted so that all alcoholic beverages were taxed equally on the basis of alcohol content and the taxes also adjusted for inflation, an additional $30 billion per year could be collected.[2] These funds could pay for all needed drunk driver control programs, with enough left over for tactics needed to deal with all aspects of alcohol abuse. And there still would be money left over to help defray the cost of national defense.

Congress, despite public posturing on the problem, is not likely to oppose the alcohol industry and raise taxes to the level they deserve to be unless grass-roots public pressure is mounted to force members of that body to come to grips not only with drunk driving, but the larger problem of alcohol abuse that tears at the very fabric of the nation. In an effort to raise excise taxes on alcoholic beverages, the CSPI recently started putting together a "National Alcohol Tax Coalition."[3]

With all of this, the President must exert effective leadership to assure that we are provided maximum protection from drunk drivers.

15

Specifically, he should order the development and implementation of a comprehensive national master plan. A small amount of the President's time, if effectively and dramatically utilized, would result in an immediate and significant decrease in the death and injury rate.

The concept of competent and conscientious task forces to combat drunk driving at the state and local levels of government has been endorsed by the National Highway Traffic Safety Administration, the National Safety Council and the President's Commission on Drunk Driving. The endorsements came after these organizations recognized the unprecedented success and potential of such task forces scattered throughout the country.

Many communities and states, after learning of the task force concept or being asked by concerned citizens to establish such units, have set them up. And in many of these areas, much progress is being made. Most community leaders, however, do not understand the nature of the drunk-driving issue or what to do about it. Many communities would establish a task force if the public officials who govern them either knew or understood the proper approach.

What the President can and should do is provide sufficient information on how to reduce death and injury to the governors of each state and the top elected offical in every city, county and town.

If the President were to go on prime-time television to address the nation on the drunk-driving issue and clearly explain the problem and what needs to be done at the state and local level and suggest the establishment of task forces, the public would respond by establishing thousands of such committees plus other aggressive efforts to bring the problem under control.

To understand its magnitude, suppose that the 25,000

who will be killed by drunk drivers each year were passengers aboard 357 jetliners similar to the Air Florida jet that crashed into the 14th Street Bridge in Washington D.C. in January 1982, killing some 70 persons. Assume that we know for a fact that at least one of those jets would crash each day killing all aboard and injuring about 1,800 on the ground at the crash site. If this were to happen, the federal government would take steps to halt the carnage. An army of competent people would be assembled by the President to work and devise methods to put an immediate end to such a tragedy.

Yet approximately the same number of Americans are killed and injured in preventable alcohol-related collisions every day, and the federal government has been dragging its feet on the issue. **Again, the White House needs to declare war on the problem!**

There is much that ordinary citizens can do to help get drunk drivers off the road. Obviously, if everyone took the time to write the President to demand that the public be protected from drunk drivers, such protection would be provided. And, if citizens would write or call their Senators and members of the House of Representatives to complain about the extremely low taxes on alcoholic beverages, Congress would act quickly to put public interest above private interest.

The most important thing the public can do is support the efforts of citizen and student activist groups that are working to combat drunk drivers at state and local levels. Some can help start or join a citizen anti-drunk driving unit or a student group in their school. The work of such organizations is vital. They deserve to be supported.

A student or a citizen activist group with a good strategy can help bring about an almost immediate decrease in the death and injury rate from drunk driving.

THE ROLE STUDENTS CAN PLAY

There are several things students can do. If you are concerned about the very real possibility that you or a member of your family can become a victim of a drunk driver (and you should be), you can take steps to protect yourself in the event you are involved in an alcohol-related crash. Use a safety belt whenever you ride in a vehicle so equipped. Safety belts are the single most effective counter-measure against drunk drivers and when used correctly will substantially increase your chances of surviving all types of collisions.

Also, refuse to ride in a vehicle being driven by someone who has been drinking. Not getting into a car with an impaired driver is like refusing to commit suicide. Call a friend or your parents to pick you up. Don't take needless life and death chances when there are valid options.

Encourage your friends not to drive after drinking. And make arrangements to have one person designated to drive for a group going to a party. The designated driver should agree, in advance, not to have anything to drink and be responsible for seeing everyone in the carpool safely home.

Support the work of the student activist group in your school, take the time to listen to what members have to say, and get involved in their work. Do not hitchhike or walk along dark roads. Drunk drivers have impaired vision, so wear light reflective clothing at night. Refuse to ride in the back of a pick-up truck or van, especially with an impaired driver. It is too dangerous.

Perhaps, most importantly, help organize an anti-drunk driving student group in your school. It takes only one concerned student (or parent or teacher) to get the ball rolling. It can help bring the teen death rate down by making sure the school is correctly addressing the issue and that the county or city in which you live is aggressively attacking the problem.

With the information in this book as a guide, a student group (or a citizen activist group) can:

- Launch significant efforts to assure that drunk driving is controlled in your community.
- Trigger a state or local task force.
- Educate the public about how serious the problem really is.
- Get the police to arrest more drunk drivers.
- Obtain more effective prosecution.
- Improve the processing of drunk drivers through the court system.
- Obtain more effective sentencing by judges.
- Help improve alcohol-abuse treatment and education programs.
- Generate public support for improved control.
- Help get new and better anti-drunk driving laws enacted in your state.
- Discourage social drinkers from excessive drinking and driving.
- Save lives and protect yourself, your friends and your family.

Remember, it takes only one concerned student or adult to get all of the above underway. The next chapter tells how.

NOTES

1. From 1981 to 1982 there was an abrupt decline in national traffic fatalities, according to the Insurance Institute for Highway Safety. Deaths went from an average of about 4,400 a month in early 1981 to about 3,500 a month in early 1983. The decline is evidence of the early fruits of the combined efforts of victim and citizen activists who have successfully pressured government for reform.

   However, the activists are generally not given credit for their accomplishment. The decline is said by some to be a "mystery." Brian O'Neill, senior vice president of the Insurance Institute, claims that "The economy and motor vehicle deaths are strongly correlated, and this accounted for the 1981-1982 downturn in deaths." This claim is made despite the fact that the Institute also reports that vehicle miles traveled during the same time period increased.

   It should be noted that the Institute does not have a record of effectively dealing with the drunk-driving issue. It should also be noted that the decline could and should have been much greater and unless the pressure for reform is increased and maintained, the death rate will return to its previous high levels in short order.

2. These figures assume that alcohol consumption remains constant.

3. Coalition members include the American Council on Alcohol Problems, the National Council on Alcoholism, RID, MADD and other organizations. The CSPI has also organized a coalition of *Citizens Concerned about Alcohol Advertising* made up of dozens of national, state, and local health, consumer, aging, youth, religious, women's and drunk-driving groups. And recently the CSPI published a book on advertising practices of the alcohol industry titled *The Booze Merchants*. Its cost is $5.95. Contact the CSPI for further details. Their address is 1755 S Street N.W., Washington, D.C. 20009.

concerned about this problem," Kim told Virginia Governor Charles Robb. "We realize it will take a while to get the problem solved, but we've got to keep working on it."

The Governor agreed. Kim presented Governor Robb with a stack of petitions containing the signatures of 5,000 fellow students.

Other student leaders and citizen activist organizers presented the Governor with more petitions that contained a total of 9,500 signatures.

The Governor of Virginia, in response to that meeting (which was well publicized by the media), established a state task force to rid Virginia's highways of the drunk-driving menace. Kim was appointed to the task force and also to a local task force in Fairfax County, where she lives. Since then, as a result of the efforts of MADD, a group now called Virginians Opposing Drunk Drivers (VODD)[1] and SADD, much positive change has taken place in Virginia. Kim continued to learn as much as she could about the issue and spoke on numerous occasions while helping organize new SADD groups.

Kim received many awards for her outstanding lifesaving work, including one presented by the Governor's wife lauding her as "an outstanding young Virginian." What Kim Ritchie did can be done in any community or state. She has written a brief set of tips to help a SADD group get started. Her address is: 4411 Westfield Drive, Fairfax, Virginia 22032.

Prior to the Virginia effort, students at High Point High School in nearby Maryland were shocked into action when a fellow senior, Katherine Sourlis, was killed in late 1981 by a drunk driver. High Point seniors Suzi Kilbourne and Melissa Kinsley organized a SADD group at the school. "Why are we doing this? Because we lost a friend," said Melissa. "But even more so, the next time it could be one of us. What if it were **Your** mother...or **Your** best friend?"

The first known SADD group in Maryland, sad to relate, fell apart after the seniors who organized it graduated.

Effective plans had not been made to keep the group going. Following graduation, Melissa continued to work with High Point students to revitalize SADD at the school. She also became the coordinator for SADD in her county, and while attending the University of Maryland continued to help make the organization a permanent and effective force.

Similar efforts have taken place in other communities. Teen-agers angered at the death of a friend, schoolmate or parent, organized and began to fight back. Unfortunately, many SADD groups are not well organized or focused. But as leaders learn the system and strategies to use, they can and will have greater impact. Despite the relative newness of the movement, many SADD groups have been successful in helping raise public awareness of the problem and forcing corrective action by demanding that elected officials take action to get drunk drivers off the road.

In Massachusetts, in September 1981, the director of Health Education for the Wayland Public School System, Robert Anastas, organized a different type of SADD program, entitled Students Against Driving Drunk. His organization mainly tries to keep teen-agers from drinking and driving.

In less than a year, the Students Against Driving Drunk program began to spread across the country following massive national publicity and the endorsement of the SADD movement by then-Secretary of Health and Human Services, Richard S. Schweiker. Before resigning in 1983, Secretary Schweiker announced that his agency would conduct a conference in the spring of 1983 to spread the SADD concept.

More than 100 schools in Massachusetts now have SADD chapters, and the movement has spread to at least 350 schools in Florida, North and South Carolina, Georgia, Connecticut, Maine, New Hampshire and elsewhere.

The major difference between Students Against Drunk Driving and Students Against Driving Drunk is that the latter stresses peer pressure and alcohol education, including its impact on driving skills. It also encourages students to sign a contract (a copy of the contract is in Chapter 4) with their parents, agreeing to call them for "advice and/or transportation at any hour, from any place, if I am ever in a situation where I have had too much to drink, or a friend who is driving me has had too much to drink." The Anastas program has attracted maximum press attention and appears to be a good approach as far as it goes. It is worthwhile to send for a full description of the Anastas SADD program to:

S.A.D.D.
c/o Robert Anastas
66 Diana Drive
Marlboro, Mass. 01752

Mr. Anastas, as this is written, is on a year's leave of absence from his school system to travel extensively to organize Students Against Driving Drunk groups. He said his presentation is available free of charge, but there is a backlog of requests.[2]

The other SADD organization, Students Against Drunk Driving,[3] works primarily to force the government to take effective steps to get drunk drivers off the roads, as well as to encourage teen-agers not to drink and drive. The preferable approach is to develop a student group that will be concerned with both concepts; improved alcohol education that is coupled with peer pressure and efforts to have elected officials do more to protect the public.

If we are to significantly reduce teen death and injury, it will take SADD-type groups in every school so teen-agers and adults can work together to bring the problem under control.

There is no question that such organizations can be effective if their leaders and sponsors learn the true nature of the drunk-driving issue and the effective strategies necessary to overcome it. It makes no difference what a group is called, as long as its goal is to reduce death and injury to the fullest extent possible with a workable plan of action.

While it is important to encourage teen-agers not to drink and drive, it is equally important to make sure all drunk drivers are kept off the roads even if it means that student groups will have to use political pressure. Many teen-agers killed in alcohol-related crashes, such as Cari Lightner and Tommie Sexton Jr., were not drinking at the time of their deaths. Simply encouraging teen-agers not to drink and drive ignores the fact that large numbers of adult drunk drivers threaten the lives of students everyday.

While copying the organizational methods of an existing student unit is an easy way to start a SADD group in your school and should be considered, taking the best of what different organizations are doing and starting a similar group from scratch should not be overlooked. With extra effort, and following the instructions in this book, you will have a more effective and cohesive working unit.

In many other communities, student groups operating under different names have worked on traffic safety issues. By and large, they have not been as effective as they might be. All existing student groups concerned with the drunk-driving issue must take a hard look at their goals and

26

strategies. An aggressive group can quickly become a powerful force in the community and help lead the way to a reduction of the death and injury rate.

HOW TO ORGANIZE A SADD-TYPE GROUP

It is a relatively simple matter to organize a student group to combat drunk driving. It takes only one dedicated person, who could be a student, a parent, a teacher or any concerned individual. It could even be you. Or two or three people can work together to get the ball rolling in your school, community or state. The only necessary ingredient is a willingness to learn strategies that have worked elsewhere. No money is required; just time and effort. The net result? Saving lives!

HOW A STUDENT CAN ORGANIZE A SADD GROUP.

If there is no SADD group in your school, the following steps will help even one student get such a movement underway.

If, after you read this book, you are willing to take the time required (at least several hours a week), the first step is to recruit friends, parents and teachers to help. Pass a note around asking friends and classmates if they are interested in forming a student anti-drunk driving group. Talk to as many as possible about the idea before and after school and during lunch breaks.

Tell them why such an association is necessary and ask them to join with you to get the group established. Give them a copy of this book, asking that they read it as soon as soon as possible, because lives are at stake. Once a few agree to help, the SADD group (or whatever you want to call your school's organization) has been started. That's all there is to it. You do not need a lawyer, accountant or anybody's permission; you just **do** it.

The next step is to approach school officials seeking their support. Make an appointment with the principal or the vice principal in charge of student activities. Give the official a copy of this book. If you are refused assistance, go to their supervisor and explain what you are trying to do and ask for their help.

Explain that the need for a SADD organization has been endorsed by the Secretary of Health and Human Services and other major agencies concerned with health and safety issues. Refuse to take "no" for an answer.

There are no valid reasons why a student group working to lower the death and injury rate from drunk driving should not be established in every school.

All that probably will be necessary is to ask for the support of the school administration, since the overwhelming majority of professional educators want to see everything possible done to save young lives in their communities. Most will see the wisdom of the SADD approach. However, if your principal will not back your efforts, circulate a petition in the school and in the community stating this fact. Ask your parents to take the petition around the neighborhood to get more signatures.

Contact your local newspaper and let the editor know that your principal refuses to help promote lifesaving efforts in your school and that you are circulating a petition among the student body and community. Ask local doctors and business leaders to sign the petition. Request that adults write or call the principal seeking his support. Keep putting pressure on the principal until he or she yields.

SAMPLE PETITION

FROM: STUDENTS AGAINST DRUNK DRIVERS (SADD)
TO: THE PRINCIPAL OF *(your)* HIGH SCHOOL

Drunk driving, according to the National Highway Traffic Safety Administration, is the leading cause of death for teen-agers in the United States. We want everything possible done to protect our lives and the lives and health of our families and friends.

Therefore, we ask your help in establishing a strong student group to combat the drunk-driving problem in our community. And once this unit is formed, we ask you to support its goals and projects.

Signed:

Name   Age   Class or Address
_____
_____
_____
_____
_____
_____
_____
_____
_____
_____

(This sample petition can be used as is or altered to meet your specific circumstances. Do not hesitate to use it if necessary. You have the constitutional right of free speech.)

When school officials have agreed to the need for the proposed SADD unit, solicit them to appoint a teacher to sponsor and work with the group. Request a teacher you know would do a good job.

Next, let the entire school know that a SADD organization has been formed, and the reasons for it. This can be done in several ways. Send an open letter to every member of the student body distributed through the in-house school mail system. Teachers should ask students to read the letter immediately. The school can either duplicate sufficient copies for distribution, or perhaps a local business or other group concerned with health and safety will donate copies.

You may compose your own letter, or use the sample letter on the next page.

Dear Fellow Students,

PLEASE TAKE THE FEW MINUTES NECESSARY
TO READ THIS.

We have a very serious problem in our community that threatens all of our lives every day. The problem is drunk driving and it has become the leading cause of death and serious, often crippling, injuries to students. It can happen to any one of us at any time. Our parents and friends also can become victims without warning. More teen-agers are killed in alcohol-related crashes than die from any single disease.

This year, 5,000 of us, 14 every single day, will be killed in alcohol-related crashes in our country. Unless concerted efforts are undertaken throughout the United States, one of every two of us, according to federal data, will be involved in an alcohol-related crash in our lifetime. This is an unacceptable risk. The majority of students in this school probably know of someone either killed or injured in an alcohol-related collision. Very often, those who are killed or seriously hurt are innocent victims. This is a needless and unfair threat to our lives that we can no longer tolerate.

We want to make sure everything possible is done in our school, community and state to protect us from drunk drivers. Therefore, we have organized a student group to combat the problem. We need your help and support. We need students to lead the organization and to work on lifesaving projects. If you are interested, please attend our organizing meeting to be held (give date, location and time). If you are unable to become involved in this important effort, please support our goals. Our sole purpose is to lower the number of people killed and maimed by drunk drivers. We know it is possible to do this by working together. Thank you.

Signed: (your student group)

Another way to let the student body know that SADD has been started is to have school officials hold assemblies to discuss the drunk-driving problem and the formation of the new group. Volunteers to help achieve the group's lifesaving goals could also be recruited at such gatherings. A film on the issue (one can be obtained free) can be shown and someone knowledgeable on the subject of drunk driving (a police officer or prosecutor, for example) might address the assembly. The students should be told exactly what the drunk-driving problem is and what they personally can do to combat it.

In Kane County, Illinois, a community just outside Chicago, a drunk-driving awareness program initiated by Dean of Students Norm Widerstrom was presented to all members of the senior class at the St. Charles High School prior to the 1982 Christmas holiday break. A presentation was made each period to the physical education classes. After the students were told how the problem affects their lives and given tips on how to protect themselves and their community, 80 signed up to be the first members and leaders of SADD in their school.

If an assembly is held in your school, or alcohol awareness programs are presented to individual classes to educate the student body about the seriousness of drunk-driving and to recruit student members for SADD, it is important to have all grades participate, not just seniors.

HOW TO CHOOSE LEADERS
FOR THE NEW SADD GROUP

There is a role for everyone in SADD. Project leaders are needed, as well as people to do the work each project requires. To assure that the new group is run effectively, it is important to select capable and conscientious student leaders as managers. The unit will need a president or executive director and several vice-presidents or deputy executive directors.

Together, the executive director and the deputy directors will form the management team of the SADD structure. The major decisions need to be made collectively by them.

It is vital to the success of the program that the most interested and qualified students be selected for management team positions. Each job should be filled on the basis of leadership capability rather than popularity.

Students who sign up for SADD should be asked (either by letter or at the first meeting of the group) if they are interested in serving in a management position. If so, they should submit an application and a resume to a screening and selection board, along with a letter explaining why they seek the position and what they will do if they are selected. When a school puts together a football team, they have tryouts to get the best players. It is equally as important for the SADD alliance to find the most qualified student leaders for its management positions.

The selection board should be made up of one or more concerned school officials and student leaders from other organizations.

When the leadership has been selected, they should meet with the school sponsor and develop their plan of attacking the drunk-driving problem.

SAMPLE PLAN OF ATTACK

1. Organize SADD group.
2. Get support of school administration.
3. Obtain support of fellow students and the community at large.
4. Start state and local task forces.

5. Work to get "Project Graduation" for this school year. ("Project Graduation" is a program to help prevent teen alcohol-related automobile crashes during the prom/graduation season. It is fully explained in the chapter which follows.)
6. Start a free-ride program to provide safe, sober transportation for teens in need (also described in the next chapter).
7. Work for improved enforcement, prosecution and adjudication of drunk-driving cases.
8. Investigate the youth aspects of the alcohol-crash problem and demand that each significant weakness that is uncovered be corrected.
9. Never give up; lives are at stake.

While the overall goal of SADD is to reduce teen death and injury associated with drunk driving, there are a number of sub-goals that will help achieve the main one. These include:

1. **Education**—making sure that every student and parent is aware of the real dangers posed by drunk drivers.
2. **Prevention**—seeing that students and parents learn steps they can take to reduce their chances of being killed or injured by drunk drivers. This includes encouraging everyone to use safety belts and child restraints and to practice such safe habits as refusing ever to ride with someone who has been drinking excessively.
3. **Corrective Action**—assuring that effective efforts are underway in the community to improve the system that is supposed to protect the public from drunk drivers.

4. **School Goals**—helping your school do everything possible to help bring the death and injury rate down significantly. This includes conducting "Project Graduation" in cooperation with SADD, plus other activities.

When the management team has been selected, a meeting should be held to get the strategy underway. Then simply follow through on what you start and learn as you go.

HOW A SADD GROUP CAN RAISE FUNDS AND OBTAIN DONATIONS OF SERVICES

A SADD unit does not need much money to operate successfully. Almost everything needed can be obtained by asking the right organizations and people for donations.

Fortunately, many businesses, government and professional organizations want such groups to be successful and are usually pleased to help if requested. But you must ask for **specific** help.

For example, if your SADD group needs 1,000 copies of a petition and the school has no money to pay for them, soliciting a local insurance office or other firm in person, by letter or by telephone is often all that is necessary to obtain them. The same approach can be taken for practically all other needs. Government agencies responsible for drunk driver control or public health may assist with photocopying or a few office supplies. If long distance calls need to be made pertaining to the work of the SADD group, some government agencies or businesses may permit student activists to use their phone facilities at no charge.

It is perfectly proper to seek donations to your SADD association. Your group is providing a sorely-needed public service and those who offer donations are not only willing, but eager, to assist. It makes them feel good. They realize you are doing them and the community a service.

In Virginia a SADD unit received thousands of free bumper stickers from local automobile dealers and an insurance company. In Maryland, a dealer donated a car to a safe-ride program.

In other places the private sector has:

- Paid the taxi fare of individuals impaired by drinking who chose not to drive home.
- Put up the money for billboards warning the public about drunk drivers.
- Paid for advertising that promoted public awareness on the issue.
- Donated funds to enable citizen activist groups to carry on their work.

Television stations have donated studio facilities for the production of public service announcements on drunk-driving, plus the air time to show the announcements. Do not overlook local radio stations and newspapers.

Besides printing and bumper stickers, your group can obtain SADD T-shirts, posters, stationery, buttons, films and literature on the alcohol-crash problem.

The amount of donations is limited only by your willingness to ask others to lend a helping hand.

If your SADD unit requires money to operate, fund-raising projects similar to those used by other student groups can be effective.

Such activities as bake sales, bumper sticker sales, car washes, or candy sales are possibilities. If large amounts are required, there are professional companies that specialize in raising money for student groups. But deal only with a reputable firm. Your school principal can identify such reputable companies in your area. Do not sign a contract with a fund raising firm before having it read and approved by someone experienced in such matters. It might also be wise to have an attorney peruse the contract. There are competent lawyers in every community who will donate time to assist a student group with legal questions. Request the public defender's office to recommend a law firm willing to provide free service to your SADD organization. Or try asking the lawyer parent of a fellow student if he or she can suggest someone to contact. You may find a lawyer you like and who is willing to work with your group in one phone call, but if not, don't give up. Keep trying and you will track down the attorney you need.

Your group should also endeavor to locate a business sponsor. There are concerned business people in your state, many of whom often donate to worthy causes and lend their influence as well. Such influence is an important concept to grasp. These citizens usually have numerous contacts and if they choose can open important doors that may help achieve the goals of your SADD unit. If you have a business sponsor who is well respected in the community and who has influence, that person or company could be a liaison between the school and business community. Find out who the influential business people are in your area. Talk to them. Tell them what you are doing and ask their participation and assistance.

Bear in mind, however, that the work to be done by SADD does not cost money so much as it does time and effort. It is more important for members to spend their time working on projects that will help save lives, rather than trying to raise money.

It may seem after reading this chapter that your task is an impossible one. It is not, but it will take time and commitment.

NOTES

1. VODD, which has 12 chapters in Virginia, started out as a chapter of Mothers Against Drunk Drivers (MADD) and later changed its name to Many Against Drunk Drivers following a dispute with the MADD founder. After threatened legal action by Candy Lightner, the organization changed its name to VODD. VODD was the state's first activist group and was first to call for the state task force. A VODD founder, Susan Midget, was appointed to the state task force.
2. Mr. Anastas has received substantial funding from the United States Brewers Association. A spokesman for the industry claims that the money has "no strings" attached to it. It is doubtful, however, that the beer industry would continue to fund Mr. Anastas if he were to teach students to aggressively go after aspects of the issue that were not in the best interests of the industry.
3. Some groups call themselves Students Against Drunk Drivers.

4 ══ ▬▬▬▬▬▬▬▬▬

SELECTED PROJECTS
FOR A SADD GROUP

PROJECTS

There are numerous projects the SADD organization in your school can undertake to help lower the death and injury rate from alcohol-related crashes.

Student members of SADD interested in being project leaders should submit letters to the management team outlining their qualifications and why they desire to work on a specific project.

Listed below are more than a dozen anti-drunk driving project ideas. Your SADD group should consider several. Perhaps you could convince a similar group in another school to undertake several different projects. Some should be done on a school-by-school basis.

THE SAFE-RIDES-FOR-TEENS PROGRAM

SAFE-RIDES-FOR-TEENS is a student-organized and operated program to provide a free and safe ride home for any student not in condition to drive safely, or for those who do not wish to be passengers in cars operated by people who have been drinking.

At a minimum, a safe-ride program should be conducted on key holiday weekends and on prom and graduation nights. The ideal approach is to offer this service every weekend during the school year.

In Anne Arundel County, Maryland, safe rides are available every Friday and Saturday from 10 p.m. to 3 a.m. Students and adult volunteers gather in the SAFE-RIDES-FOR-TEENS headquarters to man the project. One operates a CB radio and another mans the telephone. Other volunteers are paired into coed driving teams.

Each driver uses the family car, and is accompanied by a passenger who is responsible for CB contact with headquarters and keeping information on departure and pickup times, plus addresses and riders' names (required for insurance purposes).

Team members agree to keep confidential all details of their service activities. In addition, all student volunteers must complete a 12-hour training course. Adults are on duty as consultants.

A safe-ride project should be considered a must for any SADD group serious about influencing young people not to drive when they are intoxicated. Additional information regarding the Anne Arundel County program may be obtained by contacting the organization's adult advisor, Rick Carberry. His address is:

SAFE-RIDES-FOR-TEENS HEADQUARTERS
P.O. Box 151
Davidsonville, MD 21035
Phone 301 269-6464 or 261-7477

WARNING: BEAR IN MIND THAT THE HOURS OF OPERATION FOR A SAFE RIDE PROGRAM COINCIDE WITH THE MOST DANGEROUS TIMES TO BE ON THE ROAD. LARGE (SAFER) CARS SHOULD BE USED, AS WELL AS SAFETY BELTS.

PROJECT GRADUATION

Project Graduation is an alcohol and traffic safety program to help prevent alcohol-related death and injury during the high school prom and graduation period.

In Montgomery County, Maryland, one of several jurisdictions that instituted such a program in 1982, that jurisdiction's drunk-driving task force, its student government association, Council of PTA's and Business/Community Team Against Drug and Alcohol Abuse joined to sponsor the project.

Any new SADD unit should make the establishment of a "Project Graduation" a top priority. It is needed in every school. Team leaders should meet with school officials for approval and help in establishing the program. They should also meet with the business community, police and others, seeking their support. The information which follows will help you get a "Project Graduation" underway.

The objective of the project is to develop a public education effort among students and parents to increase their awareness of the dangers that accompany drinking and driving, according to Charles Short, who was the chairman of the Montgomery County Task Force on Drunk Driving.

The components of the undertaking should include:

1. Information on the dangers of drinking and driving presented to students and parents just before the prom/graduation period.
2. Reminders about these dangers during the proms.
3. Provision for free transportation home for students who have had too much to drink to drive safely, or whose driver has had too much to drink.

41

Specifically, "Project Graduation" in Montgomery County included:

INFORMATION BEFORE PROM TIME

- Presentation in all high schools of an anti-drunk driving program entitled "Scared Stiff" aimed at teenagers. According to Short, it is a highly credible and well-presented program on the dangers of drinking and driving.[1]
- Creation in each high school of a safety team composed of a student, parent and school representative. Each team was provided a safety kit that contained information to be distributed before and during the proms.
- Influential persons were recruited to address the students before and/or during the proms to encourage highway safety.
- Radio and TV public service announcements were distributed about "Project Graduation."
- The local media was successfully encouraged to write feature articles on the dangers of drinking and driving, as well as on the program itself.

DURING THE PROM

- Attractive posters warning "Friends Don't Let Friends Drive Drunk" were posted in the male and female rest rooms.
- A small tent card was placed on each table with a traffic safety message and the telephone number of the free-ride-home service.

- A safe-driving message was presented toward the end of the prom by a person influential with the students.

- Area florists were given calling cards that had a safe driving message and the telephone number for the free-ride-home service to include with corsages and boutonnieres.

- Area formal wear rental firms were also given these cards to be tucked into tuxedo pockets.

DIAL-A-RIDE

Parents were recruited by the Montgomery County Council of PTA's to provide free rides for any student in need of a safe, sober ride home. These parents were supported by local taxi companies. Cab fares were paid for by the county Chamber of Commerce and the local automobile Dealers Against Drunk Drivers (DADD).

COSTS

The cost of "Project Graduation" was covered almost entirely by donations and volunteerism.

There is no reason why a similar program[2] cannot be duplicated in every school system in the nation. A SADD group taking on a "Project Graduation" can be the catalyst in the community to get such a venture in place for its forthcoming prom/graduation season.

For additional information[3] on the Montgomery County "Project Graduation" contact:

Charles L. Short
Division on Children & Youth
200 Park Avenue, Rockville MD 20850
Phone: 301 279-1530

THE STUDENT-PARENT CONTRACT

Have copies of the following student-parent contract prepared and distributed to the entire student body. See which class can obtain the most signed contracts. Ask your school principal to have them distributed during Physical Education or English classes or at a special assembly so the contract concept can be thoroughly discussed. (If the contract is passed out in the classroom, be sure teachers are briefed on its importance.)

Prepare a similar contract for teachers and require that all faculty members sign. Ask that a copy be distributed to administrators and school board members[4] and that they also sign. Shoot for 100 percent participation.

When the contracts are distributed, encourage students to discuss them among themselves and with their parents. The contract does not condone alcohol use among teen-agers, but recognizes the reality that many teen-agers do indulge. According to the SADD unit that developed the contract, "It is a tool to protect teen-agers from driving under the influence or **being a passenger** in a vehicle operated by someone who has been drinking."

The purpose of the contract is to encourage open discussion that hopefully culminates with an agreement that will help prevent teen-agers and adults from risking their lives. It is in the public domain and was obtained from the Office of the Superintendent of the Wayland, Massachusetts, School Department. It was distributed by Students Against Driving Drunk in the Wayland public schools. You may make as many copies as you need.

44

THE SADD DRINKING-DRIVER CONTRACT
A CONTRACT BETWEEN PARENT AND TEEN-AGER

TEEN-AGER

I agree to call you for advice and/or transportation at any hour, from any place, if I am ever in a situation where I have had too much to drink or a friend or date who is driving me has had too much to drink.

Signature_____ Date_____

PARENT

I agree to come and get you at any hour, any place, no questions asked, and no argument at that time, or I will pay for a taxi to bring you home safely. I would expect that we will discuss this issue at a later time.

I also agree to seek safe, sober transportation home if I am ever in a situation where I have had too much to drink or a friend who is driving me has had too much to drink.

Signature_____ Date_____

45

PETITION DRIVES

There may be times when it is necessary to launch a petition drive. Your SADD unit could set up a drive as a project.

If properly managed, it can be a successful tool. If a governor, mayor or county executive, for example, fails to establish an anti-drunk driving task force when requested to do so, part of the strategy to force such reform is a well-run petition drive.

The petition should call on the reluctant elected official to establish a solution-oriented task force to identify the steps necessary to protect the public from drunk driving. Citizens of all ages should be encouraged to sign, because everyone (children, young adults, adults and senior citizens) is at risk.

The petition is a very effective way to mount the public pressure needed to get drunk drivers off the roads. And such drives also increase public awareness.

It need not cost any money to conduct an effective drive. All copies of the petition can be donated. Merely ask a local civic or business organization sympathetic to your cause to donate copies of the petition. Or request that a local friendly politician make the copies.

Put your name and address on the petitions so they can be returned to you when filled out. Student volunteers should put petitions (and pick them up at a later date) on bulletin boards of hospitals, bowling alleys, supermarkets, fire stations and other such public places. (Ask permission when necessary.)

Boy and Girl Scouts, PTA's, churches, youth groups and others will help get petitions signed. Set up booths in shopping centers if you have enough volunteers to man them.

Generate publicity about the drive and invite th
to request the petition by mail by sending a stamped, self-
addressed, business-size envelope for a copy. Keep collect-
ing signatures until the reluctant official sees the light and
appoints the task force.

The purpose of a petition drive is to build public
pressure—and awareness. Every signature is one more
person who has been alerted to the critical problem of
drunk driving.

When a large number have been collected, consider
holding a press conference or issuing a press release, noting
the number of names that have been collected for presentation to the official who is the target of the petition drive.
Request an appointment to give him the petitions personally.

With minor changes (name, date, place) the sample
petition on page 88 may be used in your campaign.

PUBLIC SERVICE ANNOUNCEMENTS

Television stations offer free air time to worthy groups
for public service announcements. Contact televison stations regarding their policy. If it is decided to follow this
course, a team of students should arrange with one or more
stations to produce and air student-sponsored and written
anti-drunk driving public service announcements. The
television station will assist without charge.

Your SADD organization should also have the school
broadcast appropriate and timely safety messages over the
school public address system.

Sample public service spots aimed at teen-agers:

"If you like her enough to ask her to the prom, then

you like her enough not to get high before you drive her home."

"If you have acquaintances who do a bit too much celebrating on prom night or after graduation, be a friend. Don't let them drive. You might just save their lives."

"Take her to dinner, give her a corsage, escort her to the after-prom party...and give her the car key to drive home if you decide to drink. Friends don't let friends drive drunk."

Examples of public service spots aimed at parents:

"What should you offer your kids for a graduation present? Offer to pick them up from the graduation party if their ride decides to drink before driving. Friends don't let friends drive drunk."

"When you give your kids the key to the car for the prom, remind them that responsible drivers don't drink and get behind the wheel."

Can students at your school come up with better ideas for such announcements?

SLOGAN CONTEST

Consider sponsoring a slogan contest. In Montgomery County, more than 2,500 middle and junior high school students did their part to keep their peers straight and sober by submitting anti-drug advertising slogans in a contest sponsored by the county's Business/Community Team on Drug and Alcohol Abuse.

After screening by 19 participating schools, 129 winning

slogans were chosen by a countywide panel. The four top winners received prizes at a school board meeting which was reported by the media.

The awards included two home video games donated by a radio station and an insurance company, an expensive watch from a local jeweler and two season tickets to University of Maryland football games.

The winning slogans included:

- "Drugs and alcohol, a one-way street. Don't drive on it."
- "Pot's the pits, don't fall in."
- "He took drugs, she didn't. She is. He isn't."
- "Peer pressure is no excuse for alcohol and drug abuse."

Many businesses and radio stations will co-sponsor this type of contest and donate prizes.

GETTING THE NAMES OF DRUNK DRIVERS PUBLISHED

Many newspapers of record routinely publish the names of people arrested for crimes. Very few, on the other hand, publish lists of drunk drivers. Since this is the most frequently committed violent crime in your community, the names of such violators should be made public. It's time to bring drunk drivers out of the closet.

A simple request that newspaper editors publish the names of those arrested for drunken driving is often all that is necessary. Tell editors it is important to list such names because it helps deter otherwise law-abiding citizens from committing this crime. Drunk driving is becoming socially unacceptable in states and communities where student and citizen activist groups are working for reform. Most people abhor the adverse publicity resulting from drunk-driving arrests.

The names of people charged with drunk driving are a matter of public record and citizens have every right to know who is acting dangerously and criminally irresponsible in their community.

Your SADD group should begin a project to contact all newspapers in your community and ask each to publish the names of residents arrested for drunk driving. Students should write persuasive letters or go see editors and publishers to discuss the request.

If a paper refuses to publish such names, ask why. Some editors might argue it is unfair because people are presumed innocent until a trial. (This despite the fact they will print the names of persons arrested but not yet tried for such non-violent crimes as burglary or bookmaking.) If the newspaper will not publish names of people when they are charged, request that they be listed if convicted of drunk driving, plus the disposition of each case and the identity of the presiding judge. This will alert readers to what is going on in the courts. It will also help deter people from driving drunk. If one or more newspapers cooperate, ask that they print an announcement explaining the reasons for so doing.

BUILDING A GOOD RESOURCE LIBRARY ON THE DRUNK-DRIVING ISSUE

Most school libraries have little, if any, current information on the drunk-driving issue. (Go to the one in your school and find out for yourself.) There is a good bit of such information including books, pamphlets, articles and movies available, however, from **the sources** listed further on.

An up-to-date selection of materials on drunk driving will help your SADD group keep abreast of the issue and provide information to students who desire to learn more about the problem and possibly write term papers on the subject. Teachers, if the material is available, can make writing assignments on the evils of drunk driving. The materials can be kept in the school library (work with the librarian on this).

At a minimum, write to the following organizations and ask what free material is available on drinking and driving that can be sent to your school:

The National Safety Council
444 North Michigan Ave.
Chicago, Illinois 60611

The National Highway Traffic Safety Administration
400 Seventh Street, S.W.
Washington, D.C. 20590

The Insurance Institute for Highway Safety
600 New Hampshire Avenue, N.W.
Suite 300
Washington, D.C. 20037

National Clearinghouse for Alcohol Information
P.O. Box 2345
Rockville, Maryland 20852

The American Automobile Association
8111 Gatehouse Road
Falls Church, VA 22047

Highway Users Federation
1776 Massachusetts Avenue, N.W.
Washington, D.C. 20036

MADD[5]
P.O. Box 18200
Ft. Worth, Texas 76118

RID—USA
National Headquarters
P.O. Box 520
Schenectady, New York 12301

In addition to obtaining selected information for your school library, prepare a list of free movies available. One student should maintain a clip file of local newspaper articles on drunk driving. They should be clipped and pasted on (use rubber cement) letter-size paper and kept in a file in the school library. This file will be a valuable reference source for SADD members and the student body.

SURVEYS

Prepare surveys on the attitude of students in your school on alcohol and drug use and driving. Publish the results in the school newspaper. Also, obtain a copy of the *Self-Test On Drinking & Driving For Teenagers* from the National Highway Traffic Safety Administration.

Consider promoting a self-test day at school or ask that the test be distributed in all physical education or other appropriate classes. Students need not put their names on the tests, but the results should be compiled by SADD and published in the school newspaper.

SAFETY BELT EDUCATION
AND USE CAMPAIGN

If everyone would simply adopt the habit of always wearing safety belts, there would be 50 percent fewer deaths and substantially less severe injuries in this country from all types of auto crashes. Unfortunately, only one of ten drivers uses a safety belt. There is no valid reason for failing to buckle-up. This project is designed to substantially increase safety belt usage at your school.

1. Obtain free copies of the pamphlet *How Many Of These Fairy Tales Have You Been Told?* from the Maryland Department of Health and Mental Hygiene. Write to Project Kiss, Health Education Center, Maryland Department of Health & Mental Hygiene, 300 West Preston Street, Baltimore, Maryland 21201. Phone 301 383-7290.

The pamphlet debunks common myths about safety belts. Also request copies of the *Child Auto Restraint Program: Resource Manual* and the *Consumer Guide To Car Safety Seats.* Visit interested members of the business community and ask that they pay to have enough "How Many" pamphlets printed so every student at your school receives a copy.

Arrange to have a copy distributed to all students and every teacher. Ask your principal to order them made available in English and Physical Education classes. Have the pamphlets designated as a homework assignment and help prepare a quiz on the material.

2. Before the pamphlets are distributed, initiate a survey of all cars entering and leaving the school parking lot. A team of two (one to observe if the driver and passenger

are wearing safety belts and the other to record the information) should station themselves for several days before and after school at the entrance and exit. The survey should show the percentage of students and teachers wearing safety belts when they drive on school property.

When the education campaign is concluded, take a second survey to learn if there has been any improvement.

3. Ask the principal to meet with department heads and encourage all members of the faculty to wear safety belts as an example for the student body.

4. Ask the principal to rule that no one may drive on school property in a motor vehicle unless wearing a safety belt. School buses will have to be excluded, unfortunately, because most school administrators have not yet seen fit to provide such protection to children who ride in the buses.

5. Obtain safety belt material and posters and have them displayed around school and given out by SADD members.

6. Ask the principal to obtain up-to-date films on the need for safety belts and have them viewed by the entire student body.

7. Challenge other schools to a contest to determine which can most increase the use of safety belts among students and teachers. Ask local businesses to provide prizes.

HOW TO ORGANIZE AND USE TEEN POWER

This project is called a "telephone tree" and is a communications system to alert and convince citizens to exert pressure, when needed, on reluctant or uninformed public officials. There is little or no cost involved in developing this activist tool which results in telephoning hundreds of people. Its formation can be accomplished in the spare hours of a handful of SADD members.

Assume that the leaders of your SADD group have just returned from a meeting with your highest elected county official (or city mayor). The purpose of the meeting was to request that a task force be appointed to bring the drunk-driving problem under control in your community. Assume also that the official said the county (or city) was doing as good a job as possible and that he therefore did not intend to appoint a task force and was not going to waste time reading material concerning the concept.

If that were to happen to your group, there is a method to persuade that official to rethink his position and change his mind. What you must do is bring political pressure to bear. Get hundreds of people to call or write and create an uproar over his refusal to appoint a task force. The call for a task force is supported by endorsements from the National Highway Traffic Safety Administration, the National Safety Council and the Presidential Commission on Drunk Driving.

The only valid reasons not to appoint a task force are if the community is doing the best possible job to control drunk drivers (no community is) or that the local official has his own personal plan of action that will achieve the same goals within the same time frame. If the executive does not have a valid excuse, his decision could result in you or your parents being killed or seriously injured.

Assume that the leaders of your SADD group, rebuffed by the county or city official, have a meeting and decide to put their "telephone tree" in operation. SADD leaders should then prepare a position paper on the necessity for the proposed task force, along with a release to be handed out at a press conference.

SADD leaders should then each make two phone calls. Each person called should telephone two others and soon the first few calls will result in hundreds and hundreds of angry citizens and parents calling and writing the official demanding the task force.

It will not take long for the official to see the wisdom of giving people what they want — a competent task force. The "telephone tree" has put his credibility and reelection on the line. It's that simple. Using this strategical hammer to pound some sense into the official's head is fully justified. Bear in mind that every moment of delay risks lives.

People will make calls and write letters because the majority in every community do not want drunk drivers threatening their families and will gladly take simple, no-cost steps to help bring the problem under control.

HOW TO SET UP A TELEPHONE TREE

Your SADD unit should distribute the letter which follows to all students. They may be handed out before or after school, or with permission during lunch hour in the cafeteria. Ask your principal to order them passed out in classes attended by the entire student body.

TELEPHONE TREE LETTER

Dear fellow students,

The possibility of being killed or injured by a drunk driver is something that concerns us all. Many of you have already expressed interest in helping save lives and reduce the injuries associated with alcohol-related crashes.

We need your help. Our voices alone do not carry much weight with officials whose job it is to protect public safety. If on important matters our community can speak with a loud and unified voice, officials will be forced to listen because we will be speaking the truth. Our mission to have the drunk-driving problem brought under control is a just cause.

There may be times when we must ask our parents to take a few minutes to telephone and complain to an elected official who may be ignoring us and whose positive actions could result in preventing a tragedy.

On such occasions, we will explain why you should ask your parents to make a complaint call. You also can telephone, but elected officials often do not listen to minors, even when they are right.

If you are willing to participate in our "telephone tree," please put your name and phone number on the back of this letter and return it to your class SADD representative. If you participate, you will be requested to call two friends or relatives and ask them to complain. They, in turn, should call two additional people, and so on. Each person calls two more. In so doing, thousands of complaint calls can be generated in a matter of days, and everyone involved will have taken but a few minutes to help. The complaint calls generated will not be ignored. Thank you.

Signed: (Your school's SADD group)

In addition to handing out such letters to the student body, solicit other school organizations to distribute them to their members and encourage participation. The same letter should be presented to student leaders at neighboring schools with a request that they also distribute it.

When the letters are returned, a master list of names should be prepared, with a card or form for each student who has responded. Each form should include the names and phone numbers of two more interested students. Thus, if 300 register at your school, the first name on the list could be asked to call names two and three. Name two would call names four and five. Name three would call names six and seven, and so on, until all on the list are assigned. The cards should be given to participating students well in advance of need.

When it becomes necessary, SADD leaders can then start the "telephone tree" in motion by calling the first name on the list.

If the group did meet with its county or city official and was denied its request for a task force, members of the "telephone tree" should be contacted and given an explanation and asked to have their parents call (they also can call) to complain. This would be in addition to petition drives, press conferences and the like. The idea is to generate so many complaints that the official involved could not possibly ignore the matter.

The "telephone tree" has many other uses:

• If an important lifesaving anti-drunk driving bill is stalled in a state legislative committee, the "telephone tree" can be used to generate grass-roots lobbying and complaints to committee members to "shake it loose."

• The "telephone tree" can put pressure on a police chief who refuses to correct deficient practices.

58

THE CANDLELIGHT VIGIL

There are times when it becomes necessary to show public support for better drunk-driving control. When elected officials are reluctant to enact needed legislation, a public protest can bring them a message that drunk driving is an important issue they **must** address. One such demonstration is called a candlelight vigil, which can be organized by your SADD group. Project leaders of the protest must make sure that a permit, if required, is obtained and be responsible for publicity and notifying the student body and the community that a vigil is being held.

In Maryland, victim activist leaders held a candlelight vigil to bring pressure to bear on members of the state legislature. They resorted to press releases and telephone calls to alert victims and citizens throughout the state that the vigil was being held. The first year, when the anti-drunk driving movement was in its infancy in Maryland, only 70 people showed up at the state capitol. But the next year, at the second candlelight vigil, more than 300 marched outside the capitol holding candles to commemorate the dead. Bus loads of people came from outlying areas.

The names of individuals killed by drunk drivers were read from the state capitol steps, while leaders of the vigil demanded that more be done to protect the public from drunk drivers. The event was quite effective. If you undertake such a vigil, notify the press, including television stations. Those held in Maryland received widespread media coverage, plus the attention of elected officials.

DRUNK DRIVING AWARENESS WEEK

Your SADD organization can help spark the joint effort needed to hold a "Drunk Driving Awareness Week" in your community. Leaders should arrange a meeting of concerned organizations to create an alcohol awareness week.

BRAINSTORMING

All members of SADD must seek to originate bigger and better projects to help save lives. Ask teachers and other adults if they have ideas. Brainstorm. And if you develop new project possibilities or would like to be kept abreast of new developments, please write to the author of this book, Sandy Golden, and describe them. His address is: 21 Quince Mill Court, Gaithersburg, Maryland, 20878. In this manner, your thoughts may be shared with others.

NOTES

1. The program was presented by Safety and Survival Inc., P.O. Box 8305, Rockville, Maryland 20856
2. The concept of "Project Graduation" does not condone teen drinking but recognizes that in the real world, teens will drink.
3. Also contact the National Spinal Cord Injury Association for their newsletter on "Project Graduation." They have a proposal worth considering. The address is: P.O. Box 5662, Washington D. C. 20016
4. In late 1982, a State School Superintendent was arrested on a charge of drunk driving. He was speeding in a state car a few blocks from the State Capitol.
5. Troubling allegations have been reported in the press that MADD "...has been torn by internal dissention that could hurt its campaign against drunken driving..." MADD has "... accepted a $180,000 grant from the nation's largest beer maker, Anheuser-Busch Inc., and appointed a California Anheuser-Busch consultant to the MADD board of directors." The organizations fund-raising methods have also been questioned. The practices of the national organization are not necessarily a reflection on the methods and goals of the local MADD chapters. They have varying degrees of autonomy. (See *Dallas Times Herald* article of May 29, 1983.)

5

HOW TO USE THE MEDIA TO HELP BRING ABOUT DRUNK-DRIVING REFORM

"...the press has become the greatest power within the Western countries; more powerful than the legislative, the executive and the judiciary."

—Alexander Solzhenitsyn
Harvard Commencement, 1978

THE ROLE OF THE MEDIA

The media—radio, television, newspapers and magazines—is the single, most important and powerful tool a student anti-drunk driving organization can use. It is a mighty sword to help slay the drunk-driving dragon. And it is not difficult to learn how to use and work with the media to promote your cause. Prior to mid-1980, the media in general paid little attention to the drunk-driving issue in this country. As a result, the public was kept virtually ignorant about the magnitude of the problem. Until recently, little pressure was mounted for reform.

The media failed to do its job, which is to inform the public on important issues. But that is beginning to change. Newspapers, radio and television have been sensitized to the issue, thus easing your job of getting press coverage.

Following the tragic Maryland crash that crippled Laura Lamb, the media in the Washington, D.C. area, for instance, became dramatically more responsive to citizen activists who had learned simple steps to use "the power of the press" to bring public pressure on elected officials to obtain reform.

By the latter part of 1981, a handful of parents whose children had been slaughtered or crippled by drunk drivers, concerned citizens and the author of this book (a journalist turned activist), were able to publicize the issue throughout the nation. Extensive news coverage is continuing to this day.

The tragic articles about infant Laura Lamb produced many others throughout the country. The issue took on even more significance when Cari Lightner was killed and television, radio, newspapers and magazines jumped on the "bandwagon" to publish drunk-driving stories. Currently, because we have learned to use the press as a tool, drunk driving is rapidly becoming the national priority it deserves to be and, as a result, many lives have already been spared.

Much of the news coverage was orchestrated by people when they were taught that they have access to the media. You can achieve similar success in your area.

The power of the press is being used to get the point across that drunk drivers have become an epidemic everywhere and threaten all of us every single day and night.

In late 1981, the three major television networks featured programs on the problem. Candy Lightner, founder of MADD, was featured on *NBC Magazine* telling what happened to her daughter. Laura Lamb and her mother, Cindi, appeared on CBS's *60 Minutes*, and Tom and Dot Sexton, parents of a teen-ager killed in Maryland, went on ABC's *20/20* program to tell how their son Tommie met an untimely death at the hands of a drunk driver while the youngster was on his way home from a fishing trip. Other network shows, including *Donahue* and *Good Morning America*, have focused on the issue with information concerning the work of the RID and MADD organizations.

Even the entertainment side of television has become aware of the problem. *Quincy* solved a "homicide" made to appear as an alcohol-related crash, its point being that drunk drivers often get away with murder. *Lou Grant* was "arrested" in one show to note that anyone, even Lou Grant, can be a drunk driver.

Victim activists and SADD members in all sections of the country who have learned to use the media usually obtain good coverage. This is paving the way for vigorous corrective action. Some groups have gotten the media firmly behind their efforts, with regular coverage of the issue.

HOW TO USE THE MEDIA

Begin by determining what coverage your local media has already given the drunk-driving matter. Call reporters who write about this or school issues (if reporters are so assigned), and ask to be briefed on whatever coverage has taken place. Ask to see copies of all articles done on drunk driving within the past few years. These will be a starting point for future coverage and may reveal deficiencies in the system previously documented by reporters.

Determine if your group can meet with reporters and editors to explain your mission. Build a relationship with them and whenever something newsworthy occurs, let them know about it.

Ask editors, including television assignment editors, to consider in-depth articles or video pieces on drunk driving in your community. Suggest possible story-lines, such as problems in the courts with plea-bargaining (making a deal to plead guilty for a light sentence or fine in return for the state not having to undergo an expensive and time-consuming trial), or the impact drunk drivers have on victims and their families.

In the long run, if you build a good relationship with the media you will receive good coverage. It may take a while, but do not become discouraged. For the most part, the press is now just as concerned about drunk drivers as you are and wants to cover the story, especially if there is a new angle.

STORY IDEAS

There are some reporters who would like to devote full attention to the drunk-driving issue in order to do the best job possible. But they have bosses (editors) who tell them what to do. And most journalists have more than drunk driving to worry about. The easier you can make the reporter's job, the more coverage you will generate. If you think of a good idea for an article on drunk driving, tell a reporter about it. It may just be a super idea that will result in an excellent story that will help the cause.

CHOOSING A REPORTER

Some journalists prefer not to bother talking with students about the drunk-driving problem. Such reporters are not worth your time. There are many competent ones who will take the time to listen to student leaders about a problem as important as drunk driving. They are the type you seek.

Get in touch with the assignment editors of your local newspapers and radio and television stations and inquire as to which reporters cover the drunk-driving issue. Meet with them and explain what your group at school is trying to accomplish. Request that they write in-depth pieces on the subject and in so doing research the system for deficiencies and bring them to public attention.

If you talk to enough journalists, sooner or later you will find one who will become as concerned about drunk driving as you are, and take it on as a project. Feed that particular reporter as much information as you can; it will be well worth your while.

Student leaders of SADD may receive telephone inquiries from reporters. Always return such calls promptly. The reporter may be working on a tight deadline and you must not miss any opportunity for publicity.

EDUCATING REPORTERS

Just as the public is virtually ignorant concerning the magnitude of the alcohol-crash problem, so are most reporters.

After reading this book, you will know more about the subject than most journalists. Take the time to teach them all you can. A reporter who understands the problem and its solutions will do a better job putting a story together. Lend reporters a copy of this book for background. It will provide them with helpful information in any investigation of drunk driving in your community.

INTERVIEWS

The key to granting effective interviews is **be prepared**.

Before meeting with a reporter or being interviewed on the telephone, outline all the important points you want to make. Put them in writing and if possible give the reporter a copy. Have additional material available, such as local statistics or previous articles. If you do not know the answer to a question, say so. But offer to seek the information or suggest a source where the reporter can get it.

Determine in advance what the interview will cover so you can prepare for it. Dress appropriately, always be ready for possible pictures.

GROUND RULES

When dealing with a reporter, unless you both agree otherwise, everything you say is subject to publication or broadcast. If you state that someone is a "turkey," even in jest, the quote might be printed and could damage your group's effectiveness, as well as cause needless embarrassment. Think carefully before you say anything. Make sure you understand the ramifications.

If you prefer that any part of your interview be kept confidential, work out a prior agreement to that effect. This is called "going off the record" and means the reporter has agreed not to use that material. You might also ask that he agree not to use your name in return for your information. This is called providing information on a "not for attribution" basis. It is often resorted to by public officials. The information, however, should be accurate and responsible.

LETTERS TO THE EDITOR

Writing letters to an editor about news stories or features on drunk driving, problems in the system the press has not yet covered or commenting on an editorial on the subject, are effective and worthwhile methods of keeping the issue before the public.

If you take exception to information in a news column, write the editor stating your viewpoint. This should be done immediately after an editorial or article appears. Keep the letter short and to the point; one to six short paragraphs is sufficient.

Put the most important information at the beginning so that if the editor has to shorten your letter he can cut from the bottom.

Keep it interesting and be certain of your facts. Encourage other students and parents to send letters to the editor when appropriate.

SUGGESTION: If your group is working to get a new anti-drunk driving law passed, or if you want to show public displeasure with a lenient judge, ask in your letter to the editor that readers also write to the official seeking support for the proposed bill or to criticize the judge. Such suggestions can generate a lot of mail and much public pressure.

TELEVISION EDITORIALS

Television editorials have impact. Most TV editorial writers are willing to take on various aspects of the drunk-driving issue, all you have to do is ask.

Call and discuss the matter with the station's editorial director and request that he approve an editorial position on drunk driving. (Keep in mind that the only reasonable position possible is against allowing drunks on the roads.)

Work with all local stations to encourage continuous editorials. Rich Adams, editorial director at WDVM-TV, the CBS affiliate in Washington D.C., has aired more than two dozen editorials on drunk driving during the past three years and the station's news coverage has helped sensitize the public to the issue in the nation's capital.

NEWSPAPER EDITORIALS

Newspaper editorials usually are available for the asking. Suggest subjects and viewpoints. You may offer to assist the writer with up-to-date information on the subject.

OP-ED ARTICLES

Ask the local newspaper editor if a member of your SADD group can write an article giving the teen point of view on drunk driving. This will enable you to get many of your points across. Perhaps several members could collaborate.

PRESS RELEASES

Keep press releases short and to the point. Two typed pages or less, double-spaced, is the proper length. The release should explain clearly your group's position and what it hopes to accomplish. Press releases should contain a name and phone number of a contact at the top of the first page in the event reporters want additional information. All statistics and information must be accurate. Any allegations of wrongdoing must be accompanied by absolute proof. False allegations can severely damage reputations and careers, and could result in a libel suit. It is wise to have a lawyer read any press release that contains allegations before distribution to the media.

MEDIA ALERT

When a bill on drunk driving is languishing in a committee at the state legislature, write letters to the editors of every newspaper in your area, plus TV and radio news departments, beseeching the public to call elected officials to express support for the measure. Parent activists have used this approach in Maryland several times with great success, generating hundreds of letters and phone calls to reluctant politicians.

After nearly a decade of reform drunk-driving legislation being routinely buried in "graveyard" committees in Maryland, the pressure generated resulted in the enactment of important new lifesaving laws.

TELL THE TRUTH

Never, under any circumstances, lie to a reporter or anyone else about any phase of the drunk-driving issue. You will quickly lose credibility and the entire program will suffer. Journalists can sense when someone is not telling the truth.

ERRORS

Some articles written about drunk driving in the past several years have contained errors, as news stories sometimes do. Reporters are only human and even the best occasionally make mistakes. No newspaper is immune from errors. The *Washington Post,* the *New York Times* and all other major news organizations have had mistakes in their news columns. Responsible news organizations recognize this and most will correct errors when they occur.

If a mistake in an article on drunk driving gives readers a misconception, ask that it be corrected. The first person you should call is the reporter who wrote the story. If the error is minor, either forget it or bring it to the reporter's attention so the same mistake will not be repeated. If necessary, complain to his boss.

If you are misquoted, inform the writer. If it is not an important point, do not belabor the matter. **You need the press, they don't need you.** Trivial complaints on minor points can only create animosity.

SAVE CLIPS

Save and mount for later reference every article on drunk driving in your state and local community. The "clips," as they are called, often contain valuable information that can be used by a task force (see Chapter 6).

LEAKING TO THE PRESS

There are public officials and government employees involved in the drunk-driving system who have firsthand knowledge of dangerous flaws that need to be corrected.

If someone knows of such problems but is unwilling to make the information public because of possible reprisal (many employees correctly fear they could lose their jobs if they talk to the press, even if what they say is the truth and will help save lives), let him know you will pass the information on to the proper parties without divulging your source.

As an alternative, you could provide the employee with the name of a journalist who has a reputation for keeping sources confidential. Most reporters will face contempt of court charges, and even jail, before they would break a confidence.

Very often when that type information is made public, the faults are corrected overnight. That, in substance, is what is known as "the power of the press." If you are provided facts in confidence, it is imperative to keep the source's identity secret. Failure could cost your informant his job.

PUBLICITY SEEKERS

It is relatively easy to obtain news coverage on drunk driving. But do not fall into the trap of getting coverage just to make yourself look good. Drunk driving is a serious subject and there is no room in a SADD group for anyone who loses sight of the mission or endeavors to become a media star. The press will soon turn off such a person, and your primary objective will be the loser.

GETTING DRUNK DRIVERS' NAMES PUBLISHED

Having the identity of violators arrested for driving while intoxicated publicized is perfectly legal and helps serve as a deterrent to others. No one wants neighbors and friends to know he has been arrested for operating a car while in a drunken condition.

Some newspapers now publish the identities of such individuals—in many cases as a result of citizens calling editors with a request that the names be listed in the paper. If yours will not print the names of those arrested, ask the editor to identify those convicted of the offense, the name of the presiding judge and whatever punishment was rendered. Often, people are shocked when they learn how lenient some judges are. Publicizing the names of drunk drivers, along with what happened to them in court, exerts pressure on the system and those who work in it. Such exposure can result in positive changes.

LACK OF COVERAGE

There is no question that drunk driving is a major threat to the health and safety of every resident in your state and should be adequately reported by local newspapers, radio and television stations.

While there are many issues that vie for time and attention, there is no excuse for any competent news organization to ignore a matter of such importance.

The public must be informed about drunk driving and news organizations are duty-bound to keep the public up-to-date on every facet of this vital problem.

Merely reporting the progress of an activist group's efforts in this regard or writing only about new developments is not enough. Quantity should not be confused with the quality of news coverage, especially when it concerns drunk driving.

If your local newspaper (especially if you live in a one-newspaper town), or television or radio station fails to satisfactorily cover the issue, there are methods a student group can use to bring pressure on offending news organizations.

Ask reporters why coverage of the drunk-driving problem is being neglected. Discuss the matter with the editor or news director and, if necessary, the publisher or station manager and ask them the same question. Request that investigative reporters be assigned to look into the local situation and present their findings in a series of reports.

If the media still does not respond to your pleas, launch an all-out campaign to force their support. Ask everyone—citizens, victims, the clergy, police, business and community leaders—to call and write the editor, news director, publisher or station manager, to complain. If enough people cooperate, the media may rethink its position and improve coverage on the issue.

If the news organization has an ombudsman, complain to him. Also, write to the Federal Communications Commission (FCC) and protest that the television or radio station is not providing adequate coverage of a very important controversial matter. Question the renewal of the station's license. If properly documented, such complaints can become a sharp thorn in the side of a radio or television station.

In extreme cases, picket your newspaper or television station and notify other news organizations and ask them to report on the demonstration. Implore your parents to cancel subscriptions and/or advertising until better coverage of drunk driving becomes a reality. The media should be held accountable to the public they serve.

THE PRESS CONFERENCE

Press conferences are being used to advantage by victim activist groups to obtain coverage on the drunk-driving issue. Student groups can be just as successful. But a press conference should be used sparingly and only when you have an important statement to make or a campaign to launch.

Announcement of a new student anti-drunk driving group, efforts to obtain a task force, the start of a petition drive or letter-writing campaign—all could be the basis for scheduling a press conference.

Such media events are not difficult to stage. However, they must be well-planned and orchestrated.

First, select a theme. The kick-off of a county-wide petition drive calling for creation of a local task force on drunk driving is an example.

Next, prepare an agenda. Limit the session to 30 or 45 minutes. Remember that reporters are on strict time schedules and have deadline problems.

Line up several effective speakers to make important and interesting statements. They should include the leaders of your student activist group, one or two victims who will tell what happened to them and how deeply drunk driving has affected their lives, and perhaps a respected public or school official supportive of your goals. Also, if at all possible, seek a celebrity as a participant. Pack the room with observers (students, teachers and other supporters), and line up visuals for television. These may be a picketing demonstration outside, or victims of drunk drivers. A teen-aged victim in a wheelchair usually has quite an impact on TV audiences.

In California, when that state's MADD organization went public with its demand for a task force, students picketed the capitol in support and collected signatures for a petition drive. The television news crews who covered the event had sufficient "visuals" to flesh out their stories.

Laura Lamb, paralyzed for life by a drunk driver, has appeared at press conferences in Washington, D.C. Her story was so compelling it drew national coverage, including an appearance with her mother on *60 Minutes.*

Those attending a press conference who lost a parent or a child to a drunk driver should have a photograph to display in the event that television crews want to use it.

In New York, Doris Aiken, president and founder of the oldest victim activist organization in the country, RID, has a seemingly endless scroll she unrolls at demonstrations containing the names of victims of drunk drivers. It is an impressive visual for television news crews to focus on. A similar scroll might be compiled in your area by checking public records or newspaper files.

Visuals are important to television producers, because they need more than just "talking heads" to put on the air. TV reporters need visuals to help explain their stories. Take advantage of that fact. And those who hold up a picture of a parent or child killed or maimed by a drunk

driver, or a victim in a wheelchair, present excellent
visuals that will in all likelihood be used on the air. While
this may be distasteful, it helps inform the public in no
uncertain terms of the real horrors of drunk driving. It is
one thing to say that people have been killed or maimed by
drunk drivers, but quite another to vividly portray the
results of alcohol-related crashes. It is most important to
personalize statistics.

After the theme and speakers and visuals are chosen for
your press conference, select a date, time and place. Allow
at least two weeks to get everything in order.

The best location is where reporters usually congregate,
such as the county or city hall or state capitol building. For
a student group, the local Board of Education meeting room
might be considered. In California, the MADD organization
received permission to use the governor's pressroom to
announce its formation and request that the chief executive establish a state task force.

Most press conferences should be set for about 10:30 a.m.
so the story can make the evening TV news shows and next
morning's newspapers. Radio reports, though brief, will air
immediately after the news conference, and frequently
continue throughout the day. The preferred date to hold a
press conference is usually Monday or Tuesday, because
the work week is just beginning and editors are looking for
stories.

Important Caution: Be careful that the date you choose
does not conflict with another major event. This is not
always possible, of course, since another more important
news story can break at the last minute and ruin your
chances for much, if any, coverage that day. Whenever
possible, check to see if any major event is scheduled on
the day of your conference. If your mayor or county
executive is holding a press conference at the same time,

you may not have any reporters present.

In the event only a few reporters show up for your meeting, go ahead with it anyway. You can always schedule another one later. But do not lose the opportunity at hand; you need every inch of ink and every second of broadcast time you can get.

After selecting the time, date and place, prepare a press release announcing this fact. The release form or letterhead should feature a distinctive anti-drunk driving emblem. If your group has no such stationery, borrow some from your school.

The release should contain the title of the press conference, a few paragraphs explaining the reason for it, and why it is an important subject worthy of coverage. If there will be visuals, this should be noted as a possible selling point to encourage TV attendance. The release should be well-written, with the name and telephone number of a contact person. (The press release used by MADD is an excellent example and is included in the appendices.)

The next step is to obtain a list of all radio and television news departments and the names and addresses of local newspapers. Your state press association will have an up-to-date list and will provide a copy, if asked.

A week before your press conference, mail or have students hand-deliver a copy of the release to every news organization on your list. If the list is long and postage is a problem, ask a local insurance company or other business organization to mail them. Many will gladly do so. Government agencies will also assist, if requested.

If the press conference is to be held at the state house, city hall or municipal office building, post a notice on the press room bulletin board. If reporters are present at the time, tell them about it and invite them to attend.

Contact the Associated Press (AP) and United Press

International (UPI) and request that the date, time, place and purpose of the press conference be put in their "day book." This will alert the media and serve as a reminder to editors who subscribe to wire services. Another effective method to be listed in the wire service day book is to have your school's media relations representative make the request. The AP and UPI should be contacted several days prior to your press meeting. Also send a copy of your release to insurance agencies, police departments and others who may have an interest in what your group is trying to accomplish.

After mailing the release, wait several days and assume nobody has read it. Telephone **assignment editors** on your list and inquire whether they have the release and if there are any questions. Sell them on the idea that it is an important press conference. The person making these calls should be knowledgeable on the drunk-driving issue and the purpose of the session. Try to get a commitment that a reporter or television crew will be assigned to cover the conference.

Note: Assignment editors are very busy. Some will not take much time to talk to a student about drunk driving. Be persistent (and tactful). Keep your remarks short and to the point.

SUGGESTION: Many individuals and organizations constantly vie for space in newspapers, and time on television or radio. Because there is fierce competition, the more controversial the subject, the better its chance for coverage. That's the way the news business works. If your governor, mayor or county executive, for example, refuses to meet with your group or to establish a drunk-driving task force, bring this to the attention of the media and sharply criticize that official.

Before your conference takes place, prepare a **press kit**

for journalists in attendance. They help writers on a tight deadline, and make for more accurate coverage. The kit should contain a typed copy of each speaker's remarks, a fact sheet on the problem that includes important statistics, plus a contact sheet with names and phone numbers of key people in the drunk-driving control system or experts on the issue. Include a reference to the information office of the National Highway Traffic Safety Administration. Personnel in that federal agency know the topic inside and out and can help reporters gather additional information, as well as explain the subject from the federal government's perspective.

The press kit should also include a statement explaining the purpose of the conference and the key points being made.

As noted previously, each speaker should limit his remarks to no more than five minutes. Anything longer risks turning off the press. If a speaker needs more time, it is wise to put his additional points in writing for inclusion in the press kit.

On the day of the press gathering, specify one person who will be responsible for last-minute details. A table for the speakers should be prepared at the front of the room. Reporters should be met at the entrance and handed a press kit. Do not give press kits to non-reporters to avoid the possibility of running out of them. If they are taken by others, you may miss a chance for quality coverage from the journalist who did not get one. If any kits are left over, they should be distributed at once to news organizations that did not attend.

A press event is not a time for people to get their egos massaged. Politicians who pat each other on the back at a press conference waste time and irritate reporters. Be sure your speakers stick to the subject.

SUGGESTION: Victims, in general, are the most effective speakers. Assist them with their presentations and, for purposes of television and radio, their remarks should include several quotable 10- to 30-second, hard-hitting statements. Examples:

"There is absolutely no excuse to sit idly by and allow drunk drivers to kill and maim people."

"Drunk driving should be outlawed forever in our community."

"Drunk driving is the most frequently-committed and most neglected violent crime in our community and not enough is being done about it."

"Our mayor (county executive, governor) is dragging his feet on appointing a task force."

"I've been heartsick since the collision."

"My entire life has been changed."

"What am I to do now?"

"We were so happy until..."

It is important to encourage victims, students, parents and teachers to attend the press conference. A good turn-out shows you mean business and that there is support for your efforts. When all the speakers have finished, ask reporters if they have any questions and thank them for coming.

After the session has ended, it is appropriate to call the editors of newspapers and broadcast media who did not send a representative. Offer to explain what took place and to send or deliver a news release. You must continually try to convince the media that your subject matter is important.

RADIO AND TV TALK SHOWS

Before and after the press conference, line up appearances on radio and TV talk shows. Contact the person who decides what subjects to select. If you are successful, be sure the person who will appear is articulate and well-versed on the issue and the goals of your group.

Your representative on a talk show should be prepared to explain exactly what your group is after and take the opportunity to request the audience to help by writing or calling the appropriate official to request the establishment of a task force (or whatever your group is seeking).

NEWSPAPER AND TELEVISION EDITORIALS

Also communicate with editorial writers on newspapers and television and radio stations and request them to write or broadcast editorials in favor of a task force (or whatever).

Such efforts sometimes bring positive results. **Note:** Reporters and government officials may be skeptical about the worth of a task force on drunk driving. Such groups are often established on a variety of issues as a means of getting the public off the backs of elected officials.

The reports produced are often worthless, or put on a shelf somewhere to gather dust. This will not happen with a well-designed drunk-driving task force that is action-oriented. Suggest that skeptics approach the chairman of the Montgomery County group, Charles Short, for his reaction. Rest assured, he will make believers of them. Montgomery County had a very successful task force that brought about a significant reduction in alcohol-related deaths and injuries. Short's phone number is (301) 279-1530. His address is 200 Park Avenue, Rockville, Maryland 20859.

THE ROLE OF STUDENT NEWSPAPERS

Student newspapers can play a major role in efforts to reduce the teen death and injury rate. A good one can educate students and parents to the full magnitude of the problem in your community. It can also keep the issue alive by reporting developments that occur when your SADD group begins to tackle drunk driving. The school paper can also investigate and expose life-threatening shortcomings in the local system charged with protecting people from killer drunks. If reporters and editors do a good job, student publications can be just as useful as professional news organizations.

The leaders of your SADD unit should meet with the staff and faculty advisor of the school newspaper and demand that drunk-driving problems receive extensive coverage. Considering the fact that alcohol-related crashes are the number one killer of teen-agers, it is an excellent crusade on which to embark for any serious school newspaper.

Suggest that editors take on some or all of the following projects:

1. An article about teen-agers and drunk drivers in your community. Research how many teen-agers have been killed and injured in the past five years, along with what happened to the drivers who were at fault. Thoroughly investigate the system from arrest through disposition of the case. Find out what usually happens to a teen caught driving drunk.

2. Find a young person in your community who has been seriously injured by a drunk driver and write what happened and how it affected his or her life. Or locate the parents of a teen-ager who died from an alcohol-related crash and describe the impact it had on them. A

81

doctor who has treated crippling injuries will often consent to an interview. Or a sympathetic police official may lead a reporter to the parents of a teen-ager killed in a drunk-related wreck who may agree to discuss their grief in an article.

3. Arrange for a student reporter to accompany police patrolling for drunk drivers. Report what takes place. Have police explain the problem from their viewpoint. Find out from them how many youngsters are being arrested for drunk driving and what happens to them. Are the police making any special efforts to catch and deter both teen and adult drinking drivers? If not, why not?

4. Send a reporter to a courtroom where drunk drivers are being tried. If sentencing and court procedures appear to be lax, ask the judge or a court official to explain.

5. Assume that the majority of licensed establishments selling beer, wine and distilled spirits in your community will routinely sell such beverages to minors. Survey a large number (about 20) and see if they will sell to a minor (either a reporter or another student). If any of the stores sell to minors, inform the local chief of police and ask what he is going to do about it. Report your findings,[1] and what the chief of police had to say. If numerous business places you check sell to a minor, consider presenting a copy of the article (after it is published in the school paper) to local newspapers and television stations. They may report the school newspaper's findings to the general public.

6. Investigate bus safety in your school. How many accidents occur each year? Can anything be done about them? Do not assume your school bus system is being safely operated. In Montgomery County, one of the

wealthiest in the nation, there were 244 school bus accidents in 1981. According to state officials, two-thirds could have been prevented. The county recently obtained a federal grant of $69,000 to beef up the school bus driver safety training program. Your community could have a similar problem.

7. Conduct surveys within your school regarding teen attitudes on drinking and driving, and the use of safety belts.

8. Write editorials about teen-aged aspects of the drunk-driving issue.

9. Conduct interviews with school and local government officials (police, prosecutors, judges and elected leaders) to learn what they have done, are doing or plan to do about the problem. Is it enough?

10. Investigate and report the full details of every alcohol-related death of a teen-ager in your community. Also, report on local alcohol-related collisions that result in serious injury.

11. Obtain the names of those arrested for drunk driving in your school's population boundaries and list them. Some newspapers now do this, and it helps deter people from drinking and driving. Such names are a matter of public record and your school newspaper can list them without fear of liability. Student reporters have the same right of access as professional journalists to these records.

12. When student reporters write good articles on drunk driving, send copies to the media in your community. Local newspapers and television stations often pick up such stories if they are well done, and give credit to the school.

13. Assign a student reporter to attend a rehabilitation program for convicted teen drunk drivers. Is it effective, or a waste of time? Find better programs and compare them to the one in your community. Why isn't your community doing better?

14. Conduct a brainstorming session with your group for other ideas student newspapers might pursue.

NOTES:

1. Do not name the stores unless you can prove they sold to a minor or you could face a libel suit.

6

STATE & LOCAL TASK FORCES

In each state there is a governmental system that is supposed to protect the public from drunk drivers. It consists of laws and regulations, health and safety agencies, enforcement and driver license agencies, the courts and a variety of other components and people.

The system and most of its components in **every** state is inadequate, often poorly coordinated and filled with life-threatening flaws.

States that have recently improved their drunk-driving laws and enforcement efforts have not as yet improved to the level possible. Far too many people are still being killed, even in states that appear to be the most aggressive in efforts to bring the problem under control. These shortcomings must be identified and corrected. In addition, each state must adopt a comprehensive plan of action to deter the public from driving drunk. There simply is no other approach that will maximize public safety.

Trying piecemeal to abolish or control drunk driving will only result in more serious injuries and fatalities on the highways. It is important to understand that to provide maximum protection, everything humanly possible must be done by states and communities sincerely committed to solving the problem.

The passage of new so-called "tough" drunk-driving laws will not, based on past experience, have a lasting effect. Unless such legislation is supported with proper enforcement, swift punishment, appropriate rehabilitation and intensive information campaigns to heighten and maintain public fear of arrest, the number of drunks on the road and the havoc they cause will continue.

Laws which promise more than they can deliver may appease a concerned public and grab headlines, but the price of the false sense of security they provide is too dear. Politicians who approve such statutes without reforming the entire system are naive, or simply do not care. The residents of your community must be made aware that a few new laws are just not enough.

Another common practice is to have a highly-publicized enforcement crackdown in response to public concern for better protection from drunk drivers. But unless increased police efforts are maintained and bolstered by effective criminal justice procedures, any gains made will be short-lived and the carnage will continue.

Necessary new laws and corrections to existing ones must be initiated and enacted without delay. But for them to be effective, it is important to know how the system works and where it is weak. A total systems approach should be undertaken in each state in order to uncover problems which need correcting and areas to be improved.

STATE TASK FORCES

The **best** approach is for the governor to appoint a task force of dedicated people to thoroughly investigate the existing system, identify areas that are deficient, recommend improvements and develop a comprehensive master plan specifically designed to reduce death and injury from drunk driving.

In the past three years, some 39 governors, according to NHTSA, have appointed state task forces to combat drunk driving. In many cases, they were established following the requests of citizens demanding that the state government do a better job of protecting the public from drunk drivers.

While several task forces have been a disappointment, others have not yet reached their potential. Some have been very successful. In the latter instances, anti-drunk driving laws, along with policies and procedures, have been substantially improved. Many lives have been saved. However, there remains much to be accomplished in every state. There is no valid reason for a governor not to appoint a state task force on drunk driving forthwith. If the governor of your state has not yet acted in this regard, your student group should make the creation of a gubernatorial task force a top priority.

Here is one method to use in approaching the governor of your state: Have your student group set up a committee to work for the establishment of a drunk-driving task force. Its initial move should be to telephone the governor's office and ask that a meeting be arranged with your committee to discuss the matter. Inform the chief executive that because drunk drivers pose a substantial risk to so very many citizens, an answer within two weeks is imperative. If you fail to put a time limit on such requests, government officials often tend to stall, hoping you and the problem will go away.

If the governor refuses to meet with your group, launch an all-out effort to educate him concerning the urgent need for the immediate creation of a task force. The governor may have to be forced by grass-roots student and public pressure to act. Consider a petition drive (see page 88).

SAMPLE PETITION

AN OPEN LETTER TO THE GOVERNOR

Dear Governor,

Drunk driving is a problem we can no longer tolerate in this state. Many of our family, friends and neighbors are being killed and injured daily because you are not doing enough to control the problem and provide maximum protection to citizens.

Much can be done to substantially reduce death and injuries from alcohol-related crashes. We ask that you take immediate action to protect our lives and those of our families and friends.

Specifically: We urge that you establish **a state task force** as quickly as possible (or improve the existing one) to investigate this state's drunk-driving control system, identify all deficiencies, recommend corrections and develop a comprehensive master plan to significantly reduce alcohol-crash related death and injury. We also ask that you encourage the establishment of a similar task force at all local levels of government throughout the state.

Signed:

NAME	AGE	ADDRESS

Note: when this petition is filled with signatures, please mail to Students Against Drunk Drivers at (your high school address). You do not have to be a registered voter to sign this petition, only a potential victim.

Several thousand copies of the petition will be needed. (See section on fund raising in Chapter 3 to learn how thousands of copies may be obtained without cost.)

After you receive enough copies, your SADD unit should schedule a press conference or prepare a press release (page 90) announcing that your organization is launching a petition drive and letter-writing campaign to demand that the governor establish (or improve) a task force to combat drunk driving. (See section on press conferences, Chapter 5.)

The petition should be circulated through the school by SADD members, with help from other student organizations. Have students take copies home for parents to sign. Request parents to take the petition to work with them. Have copies circulated in hospitals, fire departments, churches, synagogues, wherever people gather.

Before, or immediately after, the petition drive begins, try again to set up a meeting with the governor. Persist until you are successful. The first and only rule to obtain such an appointment is to refuse to take "no" for an answer. This holds true for every phase of work by a student anti-drunk driving group.

If the governor still will not meet with your group despite all your efforts, start a letter writing campaign in addition to the petition drive. Ask powerful and influential people in your community to request that the governor meet with you.

Many individuals and organizations will want to aid in the fight against drunk driving and will ask what they can do. Tell them to write to the governor urging him to see your group or promptly establish a task force.

If your school has a computer or someone in your group has access to a home computer that can do word processing, use it to prepare letters of endorsement to be sent

SAMPLE PRESS RELEASE
FOR A PETITION DRIVE
TO ACHIEVE A STATE TASK FORCE

STUDENTS AGAINST DRUNK DRIVING (SADD)
PRESS CONFERENCE

FOR IMMEDIATE RELEASE

PLACE _____

TIME _____ DATE _____

FOR FURTHER INFORMATION CONTACT:

NAME _____

SCHOOL _____

PHONE NUMBER   HOME _____

SCHOOL _____

A move to launch a state-wide petition drive calling on the governor to establish a task force to combat drunk driving will take place Tuesday, (date) at 10:30 A.M. in the auditorium of (name of school) (address of school) by Students Against Drunk Driving. Student leaders will ask the governor to meet with them to discuss the need for the proposed task force. Drunk driving is the leading cause of teenage death in America.
It is a situation we will no longer tolerate.

to a mailing list of concerned people and organizations maintained on the computer. With a computer, multiple mass mailings are possible with very little effort.

Obtain a list of key organizations in your area. Write them or contact them in person and request that they write letters in support of your request for a gubernatorial task force. Supply them with a sample letter (see sample in appendices). Copies of letters endorsing your call for a task force should be obtained for later use. A stack of letters from major organizations supporting your cause makes a good visual for TV news.

In Maryland, an influential executive of the Government Employees Insurance Company (GEICO), Terry Baxter, contacted the governor requesting a meeting for citizen activists who had been trying unsuccessfully for a year. Within a few days, the long-sought session was approved.

Enlist everyone you know who has clout to write or call to arrange the conference with your state's chief executive. Also, when talking with reporters, mention that you are seeking the meeting, and point out that the governor has not acted on your request. If you are quoted in the press criticizing the governor for ignoring your effort, it may put more pressure on him to see your group.

In addition, have the state senator(s) from your district and other members of the legislature contact the governor. If they will not help, inform them that all the students in your school will notify their parents that your request for assistance has been ignored and the parents will be asked to cooperate and not vote for those reluctant officials again. Parents should also call the senators and delegates and demand their assistance, as well as personally contacting the governor's office. (School officials should become involved.)

If several thousand concerned parents cooperate, it will

be very difficult for the governor not to heed the student's appeal. If your state has a toll-free number to the governor's office, distribute it to students, parents and other interested parties. Overload his switchboard with complaint calls.

If the governor continues to ignore your request, organize a candlelight vigil or picket demonstration. Arrange for students and parents to visit the state capitol and picket the governor's office and/or his home. Notify newspapers and television stations and keep them posted on progress, or lack thereof.

Criticize the governor openly. If he will not take the steps necessary to curtail drunk driving, he deserves to be taken to task in the sharpest possible manner. No matter how often you are rebuffed, **do not give up.**

When you finally get to see the governor (and you will), have a letter with you that outlines exactly what you want him to do, along with the copies of your signed petitions. Ask him for a point-by-point response to the letter. On the next two pages is a letter with examples of the things you should request the governor to do.

EXAMPLE LETTER TO A GOVERNOR

Dear Governor,

A state of emergency exists in our state that deserves your immediate attention. Simply put, our lives and the lives of our families are in constant jeopardy from drunk drivers. We look to you for relief.

It is a fact that there is a life-threatening epidemic of uncontrolled drinking drivers in virtually every community in this state.

Staggering numbers of men, women and children are being killed and seriously injured in alcohol-related auto crashes. Much of the mounting tragedy is preventable, yet the number of victims mounts steadily. Despite steps taken to date, there is no end in sight to this drunk-driving horror.

The lives of a vast number of people of all ages who will be killed or injured in the days, weeks, months and years ahead **can be saved.** We urge you to exert every possible effort to prevent such disasters. Your office has the power to accomplish this goal.

There is knowledge available to substantially reduce death and injury associated with alcohol-related crashes in this state. Please obtain and use that knowledge. There is no sound reason to permit such carnage on our highways to continue.

The public can and should be protected from drunk drivers. But it will take effective leadership from you. We therefore implore you to take bold and decisive steps to halt what has become our state's greatest disgrace.

Every day you delay means more unnecessary tragedy. We feel we are not asking you to do anything more than your duty.

Specifically, it is urged that you:

- Immediately appoint a state task force (or improve the existing one) to thoroughly investigate the drunk-driving problem and identify all areas that need corrective action.
- Decree the development and implementation of a comprehensive, coordinated master plan designed to substantially reduce death and injury associated with alcohol-related crashes.
- Endorse and lobby for an effective package of drunk-driving laws that will save lives and prevent needless injury.
- Assemble a meeting of the top elected officials of every county and city in the state and encourage them to form local-level task forces charged with investigating the drunk-driving problem in each jurisdiction from arrest through disposition and developing a master plan, so that inadequacies can be corrected.
- Encourage all police officials, prosecutors and judges to intensify their efforts to deal with drinking drivers. Arrests must be increased, prosecution must be vigorous and judges encouraged to "get tough."
- Give this matter the highest priority. We have a real crisis on our hands. Our families are not safe. We fear for our lives. Too many people are being senselessly killed.

We know that with your **effective leadership**, the goal of reducing death and injury caused by drunk drivers can be accomplished. We will accept nothing less.

Respectfully,
The members of SADD
(Students Against Drunk Drivers)

When you meet with the Governor, point out that his counterparts in other states have agreed to establish task forces. Note also that the concept is endorsed by the National Highway Traffic Safety Administration, the National Safety Council and the President's Commission on Drunk Driving. Tell him that unless he has a better plan of action guaranteed to reduce the death rate, you will refuse to take no for an answer. Make certain he clearly understands that you are speaking for students in every town, county, community and hamlet in the state, as well as their voting parents.

LOCAL TASK FORCES

In most local levels of government (counties and cities), there is a smaller system that is supposed to protect the public from drunk drivers. One exception would be a small city within a county that shares its control responsibilities with the larger governmental jurisdiction.

The local order of control is made up of police, prosecutors, judges, treatment and rehabilitation specialists and others. In virtually every community in the nation these systems are inadequate and contain dangerous flaws.

A competent strategy is the first line of defense against drunk drivers and getting a local task force appointed is perhaps the single most important thing a student group can undertake.

The purpose of the task force is to thoroughly investigate the local system from arrest through disposition, identify deficiencies, recommend corrections for the problems uncovered and develop a comprehensive plan to protect the public from drunk drivers. In communities that have partially used this approach, county officials claim death rates from drunk driving have been reduced by 50 percent or more. This means that in a county where 30 people are fatally injured each year by drunk drivers, 15 are alive today who would otherwise have perished. Further reductions are possible.

HOW A STUDENT GROUP CAN OBTAIN A LOCAL TASK FORCE

Coaxing officials to agree to appoint a local task force is much easier than having one created at the state level.

A phone call, a meeting with the mayor or county executive or perhaps a well-written letter,[1] may be sufficient. It could also take months of phone calls, meetings with officials, petitions, a press conference or two, letter-writing campaigns, appearances on talk shows and very vocal grass-roots student efforts.

In St. Louis County, Missouri, members of a newly-formed RID organization, met with their county executive. The group, led by Marge Charleville whose daughter was killed by a drunk driver, explained why a task force was needed and what it could be expected to accomplish. In less than an hour, the executive agreed to its formation.

The St. Louis County task force was very successful and helped save many lives in both the state and county. Within a year of its establishment, a front-page banner headline in the January 3, 1983, issue of *The St. Louis Globe-Democrat* proclaimed the state's "Highway Toll At Three-Decade Low." Despite the crackdown in Missouri that resulted from the complaints of victims who lost children, much still remains to be done there.

Although the feat of influencing the St. Louis county executive to appoint a task force seemed relatively easy for the RID members, it could take a well-planned strategy to force a reluctant mayor or county official to seriously address the drunk-driving issue in many areas.

As more states and communities begin task force efforts, it should become less difficult to start new ones. Have your officials contact states and communities where such moves are already underway to learn first-hand their advantages. Copies of task force reports from other communities should be obtained for reference and made available to officials in your community.

If the leaders of your community will not cooperate, use the same tactics and strategies outlined in the section of this book dealing with state task forces.

HOW TO CONDUCT A LOCAL TASK FORCE

After obtaining the promise of a task force from your elected official, provide him with a copy of what follows so he will know what should be accomplished. The first step is the selection of members and an announcement that a task force to combat drunk driving is being formed. Members should be the most qualified and committed people from all segments of the system involved in the control of drunk driving. The task force should also include concerned citizens, victims, a qualified student leader, a school official and representatives of the local alcohol beverage industry.

The actual selection will be the responsibility of the local government official, but it is proper and desirable to suggest qualified people for his consideration.

If necessary, students should join together and demand with petitions, letters to elected officials and picket demonstrations, that their interests be represented by one of their peers. After all, the lives of students are at stake and they should participate in any move to protect communities from the menace of drunk driving.

The selection of an effective task force chairman is paramount to its success. He or she could be named by the appointing official or by the entire task force membership. But it is important that the most qualified person be selected. This means the chairman should thoroughly understand the drunk-driving issue, possess strong leadership skills and hold a true commitment to the mission of the task force.

This is not the time to select a leader who has political pull or personal popularity. Lives are hanging in the balance.

STEP ONE

After members have been chosen, a carefully planned press conference should be held to announce that a task force has been appointed and what its goals will be. This is most important because it lets the community and the media know steps are underway to do something about the drunk-driving problem in your community.

The news conference should be arranged by the press relations staff of the elected official who appoints the task force, and take place at the municipal building or town hall. (See section "The Press Conference" in Chapter 5.)

Have the mayor or county executive explain why the task force is being established, and a student leader make a statement on the subject. Other students and teachers should be in attendance, as well as all members of the new task force. This would be a good time for them to get acquainted. Coffee and soft drinks could be served.

The student who speaks must seize the opportunity to explain why the student body is working so diligently to help reduce teen death and injury from drunk driving. The remarks should take five minutes or less and the statement typed and distributed to reporters in attendance.

The media is interested in the drunk-driving issue. If the press conference is not well covered, investigate to learn if the person who scheduled it did so correctly. If not, complain to the elected official.

Following the conference, the next step is for the task force to begin meeting.

STEP TWO

So as not to lose momentum, the first assembly of the task force should be scheduled soon after the press conference that kicked off the effort. Sessions may be held in the evening or during the day, with a time limit of two to three hours. Members' schedules should be taken into account before deciding on a meeting date.

Use the initial get-together to educate members on the scope of the drunk-driving problem. **Information kits** should be prepared and made available at this time. They ought to contain reports from other communities and states, local and national news articles[2] on drunk driving, and a copy of *How to Save Lives and Reduce Injuries* available at no cost from the National Highway Traffic Safety Administration. Also include a list of the names, titles, phone numbers and addresses of all task force members, as well as a copy of this book.

One or more appropriate films on the issue might be shown at the first session. *Until I get Caught* is a worthwhile film and may be borrowed from the NHTSA. Following the film have a qualified guest speaker explain the drunk-driving issue.

Members should be asked to outline problems they see with the system. The task force can discuss those problems in the future.

As a final step, assign members to such committees as:

1. Enforcement, Prosecution and Adjudication
2. Rehabilitation
3. General Deterrence and Public Education
4. Youth
5. Steering

Members may serve on more than one committee, although it is suggested that the enforcement committee be composed of police, prosecutors, judges and others involved with enforcement and adjudication.

The rehabilitation committee should consist of those involved or interested in this aspect of the problem.

The general deterrence group should be made up of members knowledgeable in public communications and grass-roots leadership, or interested in public education.

The youth committee should be composed of the student member(s), someone from the school system, members of the criminal justice system and businessmen and parents. There are no rules on how to make up a committee. Use common sense.

The steering committee is actually a "resource" unit made up of the chairman and several task force members most informed on the drunk-driving issue. Its purpose is to provide support and advice to the other committees and keep the entire task force effort on track and on target.

THE NEXT TASK FORCE MEETING

The second, third and possibly fourth meetings of the task force should be used to take a "walk through" each segment of the process of arrest through disposition of the court cases to acquaint members with the **actual** protection system in the community. The "walk through," in effect, is the first step in an investigation of how the system works.

Qualified persons from each component should make a 30- to 45-minute presentation explaining how their part of the system functions (not how it is **supposed** to, but how it **actually** works), with suggestions for improvements. The presentations should be made to the entire task force.

Besides explaining their function, the speakers should also discuss the **problems** that exist so they may be clearly identified.

At the second meeting, schedule discussions by local and state police departments, the prosecutor and, if possible, a judge. Enough time should be allotted for questions.

The third meeting might feature talks by key members of the treatment and rehabilitation functions, department of motor vehicles (on problems associated with licensing, suspensions and revocations), and an official associated with the control of licensed establishments that serve on or off-premise alcoholic drinks.

At the fourth meeting, school officials and qualified individuals concerned with other aspects of the issue could present their views.

With the conclusion of the "walk through," the task force is now ready to split into the committees and begin efforts to correct the identified problems.

The committees may call witnesses to explore problems identified in the "walk through" and any additional ones that deserve attention. At this stage, it is important for the task force to solicit input from the citizenry and from those who work within the local drunk-driving control system. Do not overlook the need for additional or corrective legislation.

In addition to the committee meetings that can take place over a period of several months, it might be wise for the task force to schedule at least one public hearing so residents of the community may offer suggestions.

When the committees have thoroughly explored each component of the system they are studying, all major deficiencies, including the need for corrective or additional legislation, should have been identified. The exposure of these problems, coupled with recommendations to correct them, will form the basis for the heart of the task force report.

While the identification of system flaws and proposed improvements will be a major goal, the most significant task force accomplishment will be the development of a master plan to reduce death and injury from drunk driving based on existing technology.

The plan should provide for the creation and continuation of general deterrence so the message gets out and stays out that **drunk driving will no longer be tolerated.** It should also insure increased and on-going selective enforcement, along with intense publicity, intense prosecution and adjudication, appropriate rehabilitation and swift punishment. And the plan should insist on "accountability:" making it mandatory that in the future, public reports be prepared on at least a quarterly basis, to show how the new program is doing. The report should compare levels of arrests with those of the previous year, as well as comparisons on all other aspects of the system. In this manner, if the program starts to slip back, corrective action can be undertaken without delay.

A critical segment of the comprehensive master plan will be the creation of "general deterrence." If a community is serious about reducing death and injury from alcohol-related crashes, increased selective enforcement must be employed on every holiday weekend, plus publicity to frighten and deter potential drunk drivers. Special programs also should be instituted prior to such major school events as homecoming and prom night.

When the master plan is complete and all deficiencies and corrective action approaches are known, the task force should prepare its final report.

When the draft is completed, circulate copies to task force members and various departments of the system for comment. Political considerations can have no place in the deliberations, nor should the possibility of offending members of the system (or task force).

When all proposals have been decided upon, include a plan and timetable for implementation and follow-up. The completed report should be presented to the elected official who established the task force, accompanied by an executive summary. It should then be made public at a press conference called by him.

This will end the work of the task force, although it would be prudent to have a small committee monitor progress made implementing the final report and provide at least quarterly (perhaps monthly) announcements to the public. If a lack of progress develops, the committee must push for corrective action, or complain to the media.

At the final meeting (when the report is presented to the appointing official), it is appropriate for certificates of appreciation to be awarded to all task force members for their participation and dedication.

WHAT IF YOU ALREADY HAD (OR HAVE) A TASK FORCE?

One of the oldest political tricks is to appoint a committee or task force to address a problem which has upset "voting" citizens. The tactic is supposed to get them off the elected officials' backs. Occasionally, some good comes from such task forces, but more often than not any report or recommendations which follow are put on a shelf to gather dust.

And the problem the group was supposed to solve continues. This must not be allowed to happen with a task force on drunk driving.

Since it is absolutely possible to reduce death and injury at the state and local level, there is no excuse for an anti-drunk driving task force to do less than a thorough and competent job.

As noted elsewhere in this book, young people should not trust the "system" or elected officials who control it to always take appropriate corrective action. The SADD unit at your school, a victim activist group, or a joint committee of student groups from several schools should monitor the progress of any task force in your state or community. When the task force produces its report, review it thoroughly to assure it did a competent job. If not, complain loudly and mount grass-roots pressure to rectify the situation.

Check the work of an existing task force with the suggestions in this chapter to determine if it is on target. How does your task force measure up? If it is not approaching the problem correctly, protest to the elected official who established it.

In Maryland, Governor Harry Hughes appointed a state task force following news accounts and citizen protests over what happened to Laura Lamb, the infant paralyzed for life by a repeat offender.

The task force helped immeasurably, and is one reason why Maryland is now one of the most aggressive states in the nation endeavoring to bring drunk driving under control. But the task force took a piecemeal approach to the problem and left untouched many areas in dire need of improvement. Innocent people are still being killed and injured in Maryland. Many of them could be saved. Experienced victim activists complained directly to the governor.

This resulted in having victims appointed to the task force, which is now in its third year and making progress.

What the original Maryland task force failed to do was take a total systems approach to the problem. Members did not conduct a thorough investigation into all aspects of the system, nor did they thoroughly review existing state laws to determine **all** of the improvements needed.

Maryland still needs more corrective legislation, some of which the governor endorsed as part of his 1983 drunk-driving legislative package.

Unfortunately, that state task force did not come up with a comprehensive master plan and also failed to encourage and facilitate the formation of local task forces. Governor Hughes should take immediate steps to correct this failure of the task force to prevent further needless pain and suffering to Maryland citizens.

A GOOD SYSTEM TO CONTROL AND DETER DRUNK DRIVERS

The ultimate responsibility for solving the drunk-driving problem must be accepted at the local level of government. It is there that society's attitudes toward drinking and driving are established, and its consequences felt most acutely.

A good system at this level will:

• Conduct programs oriented toward deterring the majority of drunk drivers who are never arrested, rather than "treating" the few who are. Programs that focus only on the few arrested will not significantly reduce alcohol-related crashes. **Deterrence is crucially important.**

• Provide for the coordination of the various functions of the control system including enforcement, prosecution, adjudication, education and treatment, public information and licensing. These functions now exist in every locality, but often fail to operate as a system because the left hand sometimes does not know what the right hand is doing.

- Achieve financial self-sufficiency by assessing fines, court costs and treatment fees so convicted offenders defray program costs. The funds obtained in this manner can be used to pay local government for increased police work, better prosecution and adjudication, and treatment programs. The burden of cost for better control and deterrence must be placed on the drunk driver and the alcohol industry rather than the taxpayer.

- Provide for system coordination by a project director on the staff of the chief executive (mayor or county executive) to provide the leadership, liaison and management decisions necessary.

- Furnish up-to-date training of police, prosecutors, judges, licensing officials, probation officers, treatment and education specialists.

- Stress strong and continuous selective enforcement by police, including the use of traffic check points (road blocks) to detect drunk drivers and those whose licenses have been suspended or revoked.

- Publicize the increased enforcement efforts and focus special emphasis on key holidays such as New Year's and high school prom weekends, which are known for higher fatality rates from drunk drivers.

- Continually warn the public through education and media efforts that drunk driving will not be tolerated in the community and that enforcement efforts have been increased and consequences made more severe.

- Provide for efficient arrest procedures.

- Assure that arrested drunk drivers will be moved promptly through the criminal justice system.

- Establish a driver record system to identify repeat offenders and make it accessible to the courts.

- Make mandatory license suspension, revocation or restriction for all first and repeat offenders.

- Supply the courts with these options for every individual convicted of driving under the influence of alcohol: (1) for first offenders—community service, stiff fines and attendance in either an alcohol education or a treatment program, depending on the type drinking problem the person has; (2) for multiple offenders—mandatory imprisonment, as well as stiff fines and attendance in a treatment program.

- Provide monitoring to assure compliance with court-ordered sanctions.

- Arrange for pre-sentence screening of offenders as a basis for selecting appropriate punishment and rehabilitation measures.

- Set prompt court hearings for probation violations. Get tough with violators.

- Stress prevention by education of tavern and liquor store owners not to serve or sell intoxicated patrons or minors, and conduct **strict surveillance and enforcement.**

- Publicize the names of those arrested for drunk driving and the punishment imposed by courts and licensing officials.

- Provide for long-term prevention with more effective education programs at schools and in communities to develop responsible attitudes toward alcohol use and driving.

WHAT A GOOD SYSTEM TO REDUCE TEEN DEATH AND INJURY WILL INCLUDE

In addition to all the components a good system must have to control and deter the public from drinking and driving, special emphasis should be placed on young people.

A workable blueprint to help prevent teen death and injury must include:

- Mandatory, up-to-date, relevant alcohol and other drug abuse education starting at the kindergarten level and continuing through senior high school and college.

- The establishment and support of SADD groups in all schools and colleges.

- Programs such as "Project Graduation" and providing safe, sober rides for teens.

- Promotion of the correct use of safety belts at all times.

- Energetic enforcement of alcohol beverage laws to prevent sales to minors and drunks.

- Selective enforcement and aggressive publicity aimed at teen drinking drivers.

- Forceful prosecution and adjudication of arrested teen drivers.

- Severe punishment and sanctions.

- Treatment and education programs designed specifically for teens who are abusing alcohol or other drugs (alcohol is a drug). Teens should not attend "adult" education and treatment programs.

- Suspending drivers' licenses of teen-agers convicted of drunk driving and withholding them pending completion of court-ordered education and/or treatment.

• Community awareness programs to constantly remind teen-agers and parents of the dangers of driving after drinking, and the legal consequences thereof.

THE CURRENT SYSTEMS
IN STATES AND COMMUNITIES

The systems (police, prosecutors, courts, education and treatment) in all states and most communities concerning drunk drivers are deficient, frequently uncoordinated and often loaded with dangerous flaws which result in many preventable deaths and injuries. The systems vary in each state, county, city and town. That is why a separate task force approach is necessary at every level of government. While many of the problems are general in nature, the only way to uncover specific ones is by a thorough local investigation.

Deficiencies and flaws can include:

• Inadequate state laws.

• A poor record-keeping system by a state department of motor vehicles that makes it impossible to know when a person is a repeat offender. The failure of courts to send records of convictions to motor vehicle agencies.

• Weak enforcement of alcohol beverage and drunk-driving laws by state, county and city police.

• Lax prosecution efforts, routine plea-bargaining, reduction of alcohol-related offenses to a non-alcohol related offense and inadequate time for case preparation by lazy prosecutors.

• Inadequate training of police, prosecutors and judges.

• Probation violations that are ignored.

• Dangerously-slow adjudication. (In Montgomery County, a local task force found that DWI offenders were routinely being arrested for a second offense without having gone to trial on the first. One driver was arrested a fourth time without having been tried on three prior arrests.)

• Antiquated arrest and processing procedures.

• Failure to use selective enforcement policies.

• Insufficient use of publicity to warn the public that stronger enforcement efforts are underway and convictions have increased.

• Courts routinely sending repeat offenders to the same education programs five and six times.

• Failure to monitor convicted drunk drivers to insure that they comply with court orders.

• A refusal to issue driver license suspensions or revocations.

The list is endless. Every system must be thoroughly checked and existing problems corrected. There is no other way.

The next chapter will explain how to investigate the system.

NOTES

1. See sample in appendices.
2. Often, a state or local office of the Department of Motor Vehicles, a police department media office or another agency will have news clips on the issue. They can be photocopied and disseminated to point out existing problems in the system.

7

THE DRUNK-DRIVER
CONTROL SYSTEM

In virtually all communities, the system established to protect people from drunk drivers is not effective. There are many reasons why this is true.

To investigate the system thoroughly, it is necessary to understand both the drunk-driving problem and how the various components of the system function and interrelate.

The following section on components of the system is intended as a guide to help motivated individuals understand and undertake the investigative process. It should be used by activist groups and task force members. It is not intended as a blanket condemnation of police, prosecutors, courts or others involved in the drunk-driver control system.

There are dedicated and concerned workers in each part of the system, and there may be valid reasons why they fail to do a better job of protecting the public from drunk drivers. They deserve fair and courteous treatment from student and citizen activist groups and task force members. Keep an open mind when scrutinizing the system in your area. But do not be afraid to criticize publicly and demand corrective action when flaws or problems are uncovered; it may be vital to public safety to do so.

Ask tough questions, but be fair. Allow officials and workers in the various agencies to tell their side of the story.

When problems are discovered, learn why they are not being corrected.

THE POLICE

Police officers are key elements of the control operation. In most communities, they are a major part of the breakdown that allows uncontrolled drunk driving to take place.

As a general rule, police arrest very few drunk drivers. Occasionally, they even "look the other way" when they spot a motorist under the influence. As noted earlier, the average policeman arrests less than five drunk drivers a year (according to federal data).

Some motorists have driven while intoxicated dozens of times a year for 10 to 15 years without being caught. It is claimed that for every drunk driver arrested by police in many areas, another 500 to 2,000 are not. The result of this lax enforcement is that the drinking public has little or no fear of arrest for driving while impaired. Without such concern, there is a lack of general deterrence, and the problem remains uncontrolled.

Using existing resources, police could catch substantially more violators. But such arrests are not made because of a variety of problems. They include:

- Lack of attention by police leadership to the drunk-driving problem.

- Inadequate training of officers regarding the detection and proper arrest of alcohol-impaired drivers.

- Antiquated or cumbersome arrest procedures.

112

• Too much individual police discretion about whether or not to arrest a drunk driver.

• Lack of sufficient state-of-the-art alcohol breath-testing devices and trained operators.

• Not enough public demand and support for police to catch and deter drunk drivers.

• Insufficient police public relations programs and the lack of vigorous selective enforcement to foster general deterrence.

• The feeling (not without just cause) that nothing meaningful will happen in court to drunk drivers.

The list of problems within the law enforcement segment of the control system is lengthy and different for each police department. Activist groups must determine exactly how police deal with drunk drivers in hopes of uncovering major areas which demand correction.

HOW TO EXAMINE THE POLICE ROLE

The policies and procedures used in drunk-driving control by all law enforcement agencies (state, city and county police and the sheriff's department) operating in the jurisdiction under review should be separately investigated.

It may be that the police are doing an outstanding job. If so, they deserve to be praised. But if arrests are lower than they should be, based on the estimated number of drunk drivers on the road, it is necessary to find out why.

Start by asking the chief of police or other ranking officer to outline department policies and strategies for drunk-driver control. Arrest procedures should be explained and questions concerning the department's role answered.

Determine the number of arrests annually by each department and each officer. Could more apprehensions be made using existing resources? What specific problems stand in the way of increasing arrests? What other problems does management see that hinder effective drunk-driver control?

Besides explaining verbally how the department functions, a list of all known problems with drunk-driver control should be submitted in writing to the activist group or task force, along with suggestions for corrective action. The list of problems should not be limited to the police function. If difficulties exist in the courts, the prosecutor's office or elsewhere, they should also be identified.

Any changes in police procedures in the drunk-driving area that may have affected arrests also bear explanation.

Review copies of police training materials, as well as copies of written procedures and standing orders on drunk-driving control. Also review any agreements that may exist between police and prosecutors.

Meet and talk with police officers who make drunk-driving arrests, especially those who lead in that category. Ask why they make so many, while others make so few.

Attempt to identify officers who **could** make more arrests, but choose not to do so. Ask them to explain.

Request that judges, prosecutors and others who have contact with the police to comment on their handling of such arrests.

Encourage members of the police force to bring to the attention of the student activist group or task force any problems that pertain to the drunk-driver issue.

Appeal to such police unions as the FOP (Fraternal Order of Police) to provide input to the task force process. The Teamsters Union also represents some police departments; its comments could be invaluable.

Circulate a questionnaire to all police requesting input. It is not necessary that they sign their name. Attach a notice to the questionnaire explaining the mission and goal of your group.

Questions to ask police:

• Are there problems with state or local laws that hinder your efforts to control drunk drivers?

• Do any departmental policies prevent more arrests? Explain.

• What difficulties have been observed in the prosecutor's handling of drunk-driver cases?

• What are the problems in the courts? Are one or more judges particularly lenient? Why?

• Are you discouraged from making drunk-driving arrests? What is the attitude of the chief of police?

• Do you know of difficulties with procedures relating to convicted drunk drivers who violate probation? Be specific and offer examples.

• Are alcoholic beverages being sold to minors and are intoxicated people often served at local bars and restaurants? What is or is not being done to enforce alcohol beverage laws?

• What suggestions do you have for improvements?

When the questionnaires are returned they must be carefully read and analyzed. Problems identified should be compiled and a written report submitted to the task force and released to the media.

If any life-threatening matters are uncovered that demand immediate action, see that they are brought to the attention of proper authorities.

Responsible chiefs of police who sincerely desire to see drunk driving curtailed should not mind if their officers respond to a drunk-driving questionnaire. The procedure is an attempt to improve public safety—not to point the finger of blame at anyone. Unless inadequacies are rooted out, they will never be corrected.

Note: Increased participation by police officers can be expected if you have the chief of police encourage them to fill out the questionnaire.

WHAT IS AN EFFECTIVE LEVEL OF ENFORCEMENT?

No one can accurately predict just how many drunk drivers need to be arrested to serve as an effective public deterrent. With such apprehensions standing at less than five per officer per year, it would not be difficult to double or quadruple the number. In most communities it is a simple matter for trained enforcement officers to arrest dozens of drunk drivers a year. If it ever becomes difficult for trained officers to find such violators, it is apparent that the proper level of arrest has been reached.

NHTSA research reveals that in communities where enforcement is lax, 2,000 intoxicated drivers escape detection for every driver arrested. Where it is vigorous, this figure drops to 500. Selective enforcement, continuous publicity and swift punishment will decrease these totals even further.

HOW TO GET BETTER ENFORCEMENT

If police can be made to arrest increased numbers of drunk drivers and keep the public informed of their activity, many impaired people will stay off our streets and highways for fear of being caught.

Meet with the chief of your police department and ask for increased enforcement efforts and the use of traffic checkpoints (roadblocks) as possible deterrents.

Request that all drivers involved in hazardous moving violations or collisions be tested by a reliable breath-alcohol screening device or other chemical analysis for alcohol. Publicize such changes in enforcement when they occur.

Also seek to have all fatal and serious injury alcohol-related crashes thoroughly investigated, including events preceding the incident. Police should determine where such drivers did their drinking. If a tavern or bar in the community has a history of serving people who are intoxicated, selective enforcement must be used to bring the establishment into compliance with the law.

In many communities police already know which are the problem bars, but choose to let them operate. This is a dereliction of the police department's duty. Determine if police in your area enforce alcohol beverage laws properly, or in a catch-as-catch-can manner.

Demand that forceful, well-publicized patrols be conducted in areas of high DWI activity and crash experience. Traffic checkpoints and aggressive enforcement can keep many drunk drivers off the roads. A 500 to 1000 percent increase in arrests is not impossible because of existing abysmally-low rates. When police start doing what they should have been doing all along, substantial, positive change takes place almost at once.

The word will circulate in the community that drunk-driving laws **are** being enforced and chances of arrest are substantially greater. As a consequence, drunk driving will decrease. However, if enforcement slackens or problems develop in other parts of the system to render the arrests meaningless, drunk driving and all its consequences will rebound.

When selective enforcement techniques are being used this fact should receive continuous publicity. The police should issue weekly news releases informing the public of their efforts and warning that drunk drivers will be apprehended and charged. They should also stress the constant need for zealous enforcement of alcohol beverage laws and keep bars, taverns, restaurants and liquor stores under close surveillance.

Special publicity programs should be launched on holiday weekends. Have police announce the number of drunk drivers arrested the previous week and the results of current court cases. Gear such announcements for broadcast on a Friday as a reminder to the public that the odds of arrest for this offense have greatly increased.

Police should always remind the public in these announcements to wear safety belts and use child restraints. This barrage of deterrent drunk-driving publicity and reminders to buckle up will help change the public attitude, which is an important part of the solution to the drunk-driving problem.

Unless police employ energetic public information campaigns, attempts to control drunk drivers will have only a short-term effect. Aggressive activity must be a permanent strategy for all police departments. A temporary crackdown to appease a concerned citizenry is irresponsible.

It is imperative to understand that if every drunk driver arrested in 1981 had been imprisoned, the fatality rate in 1982 would have dropped only by one percent, according to the NHTSA. This is because there are so many drunk drivers on the highway. Bear in mind that the average DWI violator may drive in an intoxicated condition about 80 times a year for nearly four years before being arrested. Thus police must create and maintain general deterrence.

There is a new device all police departments should acquire to aid in the detection of alcohol-impaired drivers. It is a **preliminary breath-test** apparatus (PBT) which can be used at the roadside to screen for alcohol impairment.

About the size of a package of cigarettes, it permits an officer to make an accurate determination of a driver's blood alcohol content from a breath sample. State laws may have to be changed to allow for its use. It would replace the highly inaccurate "field sobriety test" in which a police officer has a suspected drunk perform a variety of tests, such as walking a straight line and touching the nose with the tip of a finger with eyes closed. Field sobriety tests can be, and often are, foiled by alcoholics and problem drinkers who have developed a tolerance to intoxicants. You can't fool a properly used PBT.

Ask that a budget be prepared and submitted to the proper authority indicating what continuous enforcement efforts will cost. But note that positive results can also be realized from good management techniques without new funding in most police departments. It is simply a matter of setting preferences and learning to manage resources more effectively.

Drunk driving deserves the highest priority from your police force. If the public demands that drunk driving have a high priority, the police department will respond.

SUGGESTION: Have police obtain more information on PBT's and other enforcement and training tools. Contact the NHTSA for details.

PROSECUTION

In many cases, prosecutors fail to protect the public from chronic drunk-driving offenders. They have many excuses. Obviously, not all of them handle drunk-driving cases negligently. But many do. Any let-down in the prosecutor's office can lead to inappropriate or inadequate punishment.

When this occurs, it is a symptom of bad management and displays a lack of understanding regarding the extreme importance of the alcohol-crash problem. In isolated cases, poor protection may stem from a prosecutor who himself has a drinking problem and, out of self-interest, fails to do his job.

Inadequate prosecution has a devastating effect on the local drunk-driving control system. Those who over-imbibe soon learn that they can get away with drunk driving even when arrested. With no deterrence by punishment the evil persists along with its companions — death and injury. In addition, where prosecution is lax, police make fewer arrests because of frustration and the knowledge that the drunk drivers they do apprehend will, in most cases, get off almost scot-free.

Improved effort must be exerted by any prosecutor's office lax in handling drunk-driving cases; all it takes is an honest commitment from the boss.

Prosecutorial problems can include:

• Inadequate training and seasoning of the assistants who actually handle drunk-driving cases in court.

• Not enough time for assistant prosecutors to prepare cases.

• Routine plea-bargaining from a drunk-driving charge to a lesser non-alcohol-related charge to speed up cases and clear court dockets. This practice is a dangerous rip-off and should be halted. It results in such offenses being repeated.

• Lack of written guidelines and clear-cut policies for assistant prosecutors to follow.

• Failure to screen convicted drunk drivers with alcohol-abuse assessments before sentencing so proper punishment, education, treatment or other meaningful preventative sanctions can be invoked.

• Failure to have available the complete driving record of

the person charged at time of trial, plus insufficient pre-sentence investigations.

- Existence of an attitude among the prosecutor's staff that such cases are routine traffic offenses and should be handled as such. Drunk driving is an intentional, willful act and a life-threatening crime. Prosecutors need to recognize this fact.

- Neglecting to work closely with victims and to keep them informed concerning fatality and serious injury cases.

- Failure to obtain and present impact statements of victims as part of the pre-sentence evidence or to use public relations efforts, to foster community awareness and general deterrence.

HOW TO INVESTIGATE FOR INEFFECTIVE PROSECUTION

Investigating the prosecutor's role in the drunk-driver control system requires knowing the right questions to ask. Ask the prosecutor and his assistants to explain their system and procedures, outline problems in the office and other parts of the system which affect the handling of drunk-driver cases in the courts and offer recommendations for corrective measures.

Copies of office guidelines regarding such proceedings should be made available to activists and the task force.

Questionnaires like the ones for the police department should be presented to all members of the prosecutor's staff. Query judges, police, probation officers and victims as to complaints or problems in the prosecutor's office which they feel need rectification.

Determine the number of drunk drivers arrested during the past several years and the dispositions of their cases. How many charges were dropped? How many of the original number convicted? How many convictions appealed? What happened to the appeals? How many were dropped on appeal? How many plea-bargained to a lesser offense? How many were convicted but will not have a record of the offense posted to their driver license?

Does the chief prosecutor personally review all cases that are disposed of without being tried? Does he check fatal and serious personal injury cases to ascertain if they are vigorously prosecuted? Are victim impact statements utilized in the sentencing process?

Do not take the chief prosecutor's word for what is happening. Sometimes they are not completely honest when discussing their competence and performance on the job. We all tend to evaluate our job performance favorably. Therefore, let the record speak for itself.

Are repeat offenders singled-out for special treatment? Are all cases screened to identify repeat offenders?

SADD members should be encouraged to visit the courts and observe how actual trials are conducted by judges, prosecutors and defense lawyers.

Seek to determine any policy or procedure changes that were made in the past year relating to drunk-driver prosecution, and if the prosecutor's staff has problems with police or judges. Talk to reporters who regularly cover the courts for their opinions and observations. They can be a gold mine of useful information.

Ask the prosecutor for an estimate of funds necessary to correct any existing problems.

HOW TO ACHIEVE
MORE EFFECTIVE PROSECUTION

Request the elected prosecutor (he or she may be called a state's attorney or district attorney) to assess how the office handles drunk-driving cases. Try to get a commitment that the office will prosecute drunk drivers to the fullest extent of the law.

Ask that alcohol-related offenses not be plea-bargained to such minor charges as driving with a defective muffler (this actually happened) or a non-alcohol related charge. Such nonsense encourages repeat offenders to stay on the road. The second time an individual is caught driving drunk should serve as a red warning flag that such people cannot control their actions and are needlessly endangering public safety. Repeat offenders should have the "book" thrown at them.

The state's attorney must let people know that drinking and driving will not be tolerated in his community and that there will be no exceptions.

VICTIM IMPACT STATEMENTS

When sentencing drunk drivers who have been found guilty of injuring or killing someone, it is not unusual for judges to be unaware of the terrible impact such drivers have had on the lives of others. When judges know the complete story, they often sentence differently.

A written explanation of such matters should be filed with the court in all cases involving loss of life, serious injury or extensive property damage. The victim impact statement helps judges understand the seriousness of the crime committed. It should be prepared by the victim, his family or their attorney.

It should be the prosecutor's responsibility to obtain and submit to the courts the impact statement after the conviction and before sentencing takes place.

THE VICTIM'S RESPONSIBILITY

Typically, in the United States, victims are encouraged by their civil attorneys to stay away from the criminal proceedings of their case. They are told that the state will take care of it. This is bad advice and should be ignored. Prosecutors often do a disappointing and inadequate job prosecuting drunk-driving cases that involve tragedy.

It is important, therefore, that victims press the prosecutor to correctly handle their case. Demand to be kept informed on each step of the proceedings. Attend every hearing and the trial. The victim has not only the moral right, but a need, to know what is happening in his case.

Victims should consider joining or establishing a local citizen activist group such as MADD, RID or SADD to guarantee that the crime of drunk driving is adequately dealt with by the system.

JUDGES AND COURTS

Judges and the courts in which they serve receive the most severe criticism regarding their roles in the drunk-driver control system. Too often, the complaints are justified and the criticism is well deserved.

Most judges in this country are too lenient in their sentencing of drunk drivers. Many routinely allow plea-bargaining arrangements that are not in the public interest.

Chronic repeat offenders are not viewed by some judges as the dangerous criminals they are and thus receive meaningless, informal probations. Many continually break the conditions of probation placed by judges, yet little, if any, action is taken against them. It is not unusual for an individual on probation for an alcohol-related charge to kill or maim while driving in an intoxicated condition. Too many of our courts and the judges who run them are, in effect, ignoring the problem or are not aware of its severity. Some courts are understaffed and unable to cope. There may also be other problems. Some jurists use such legal schemes as "deferred sentencing" and "probation before judgment" to speed up dockets. Purposefully or not, such tactics give drunk drivers a break. As a result, the public suffers. These judges are indulging in a dangerous practice that enables such motorists to continue driving while under the influence of alcohol.

In some court systems it is possible to "buy" your way out of an alcohol-related charge. This is not in any way to imply that judges can be bribed (although some can and have been caught). It means that by hiring an expensive defense attorney who knows his way around the system, who demands a jury trial, who always appeals the case and who seeks continuances to cause delays, it is often possible to get the case dismissed or plea-bargained to a lesser offense.

Judges do not always receive pre-sentence investigations on convicted drunk drivers. At the time of sentencing, he may have incomplete records that do not indicate the person before him is a repeat offender.

Alcoholics, problem drinkers, even social drinkers who drive while impaired must be treated in a vastly different manner by the courts. Without alcohol-abuse assessments, pre-sentence investigations or complete driver records, judges cannot usually render the proper sentence. This jeopardizes public safety by giving chronic drunk drivers the impression that drinking and driving is not a very serious offense, at least from the court's perspective.

The major reason most judges do not succeed in protecting the public from drunk drivers is that most of them are **not well-informed** concerning the dynamics of the matter and, therefore, do not understand the vital role they must play in the control system. Judges need in-service training on the alcohol-crash problem, as do school teachers and others.

Mistakes and mishandling of drunk-driving cases by well-meaning but uninformed judges often cost innocent people their lives.

HOW TO MAKE COURTS MORE EFFECTIVE

There is much room for improvement in the manner the courts process drunk drivers. Judges react to public pressure and criticism and will change their habits if the public demands it.

The initial move is to learn what is actually going on in the courts. This can be accomplished by auditing records or simply sitting in court and observing. The results should be made public through the media.

Student and citizen activist groups must make judges understand that they are expected to play a key role in creating general deterrence. Unlike most other forms of violent crime, drunk driving can be largely prevented. SADD leaders should meet with judges and their assistants and seek more effective processing of drunk drivers. Help judges who handle these cases realize the extent of the alcohol-crash problem and suggest that competent judicial training on this matter be mandatory for all members of the bench.

When a local task force is established, one or more judges should be members. They should explain how the system works from their perspective and the problems they see in the total system, with recommendations for improvement.

126

COURT RECORDS

Court records of drunk-driving cases are public documents and anyone has a legal right to view them. The task force and/or activist groups should audit these records. Volunteers of any age can be trained to do this.

The audits will reveal what methods each judge usually employs when sentencing drunk drivers and will indicate how the courts are operating. They also may bring to light existing deficiencies in the processing and sentencing of convicted drunk drivers.

The audits should examine what happens to such drivers on first and subsequent arrests, and the sentence patterns of each judge. Release the information gathered to the media.

THE JURY

Judges and prosecutors often claim that juries will not convict drunk drivers because most people have at one time or another driven while under the influence of alcohol. "There but for the grace of God go I," is the thinking of the average juror, they argue. This is absolute nonsense. Do not ever buy that argument; it is but an attempt to shift the blame of ineffective prosecution and court processing to the public.

When people are sensitized to the magnitude of the drunk-driving problem, juries will convict. Potential jurors must be convinced that "There but for the grace of God goes my child or loved one who was killed or injured by a drunk driver." In areas where public awareness has been raised by activists, juries are convicting drunk drivers and judges are sentencing them to prison terms.

EFFECTIVE COURTS

An effective court system is one in which judges are educated to understand the alcohol-crash problem and the role they must play in protecting the public from repeat offenders.

Such courts will provide meaningful punishment and sanctions, and will order treatment and alcohol education.

As a companion to efficient case processing, jurists must order pre-sentence investigations for all convicted drunk drivers to determine the best mix of punishment, sanctions and treatment. Without such data, it is almost impossible for judges to impose proper sentences that best serve the public interest.

Judges should also insist that all alcohol-related offenses be included in the driver's record.

The courts should make the public aware of their tough stance regarding drunk drivers. Their message should be that the courts will not tolerate such offenses. Judges, too, could schedule a press conference in the interest of general public deterrence.

They should also be requested to bring any problems with state law, processing by prosecutors, or police to the attention of legislative and administrative authorities.

ALCOHOL-ABUSE ASSESSMENTS

Every convicted drunk driver should undergo an alcohol-abuse assessment before sentencing to determine the nature of the drinking problem that led to his arrest so proper punishment and sanctions can be imposed. The cost should be borne by the person charged.

A social drinker should receive different sanctions than

someone with a severe drinking problem. Currently, the majority of convicted drunk drivers are not assessed. This is a serious weakness.

Check the sentencing practices of judges to determine whether they are using pre-sentence alcohol-abuse assessments and whether or not the system provides that the drunk driver assume the expense.

Shortcuts only compound the problem and lead to repeat offenses, loss of lives and more injuries.

COURT MONITORING

What is happening in the courts? Are they effective? Are judges too lenient? Do they routinely approve dangerous plea-bargaining arrangements? Are prosecutors prepared with their cases when they go to trial and do they perform well in the courtroom? Do repeat offenders often receive probation? Do the prosecutors object?

Can alcohol-related convictions be expunged from the record? Are pre-sentence alcohol-abuse assessments being used? Is judge and court "shopping" going on? Are numerous delays granted in drunk-driving trials?

Are victim impact statements available to help determine more appropriate sentencing? Are drunk-driving charges often dismissed without going to trial? Are they dismissed on appeal? Are probation violators returned to the court and punished, or merely given more probation?

Determining the answers to these questions and publicizing them is vital to public safety.

As previously stated, an effective means of learning what is going on is to sit in the courtroom observing drunk-driving trials and recording how the cases are handled. This is called **court monitoring.** It can be very effective.

All student activist groups should take this approach so they can bring pressure to bear for improved court procedures regarding drunk drivers.

Every judge who handles such cases should be court monitored. Those who deal effectively with convicted drunk drivers help deter others. Those jurists welcome court monitors and will sometimes meet with activists to explain their procedures.

Unfortunately, there are some judges who view their courtroom as a kingdom and resent any intrusion. And judges who render questionable decisions will be outraged over any adverse publicity citizen and student activist groups may generate when they give the results of their court monitoring to the media. But using this method to expose questionable or negligent court practices is necessary to bring about reforms, so do not be intimidated by judges. They are public servants and the public has a right to observe their work.

The volunteers who do court monitoring should be trained to understand what they observe and to record their findings properly.

Issue a press release on your intentions to monitor the courts and send a letter to each judge. (See sample letter in the appendices.)

SUGGESTION: Court monitoring is a very effective method of fostering immediate improvements. But to be effective, it must be well-organized. Solicit the assistance of the local League of Women Voters, PTA's, service clubs, senior citizen groups and such civic-minded organizations as the American Association of University Women to help staff the project.

CAUTION: While ferreting out specific problems in your court system, it is also important to ask judges their views on the matter.

PROBATION

Convicted drunk drivers, even those who caused a death, are often granted probation in lieu of jail or heavy fines.

In far too many instances, probation terms are violated and nothing happens. Some court systems either ignore the fact that probation violations have taken place or are not aware of them. Regardless of the cause, or who is at fault, such problems must be corrected.

The conditions of probation that are violated usually include continuing to drive while intoxicated, operating a motor vehicle with a suspended or revoked license, and failing to attend mandated treatment or alcohol education programs.

Every probation violation must be promptly reported and acted upon. Ignoring probation violations is a serious matter and poses an unnecessary threat to society.

Any convicted drunk driver who is on probation and disregards conditions laid down by the judge is a menace and must be returned to court so appropriate action can be taken before he kills or maims someone.

Trace the steps taken when probation is violated and what, if anything, prosecutors and courts do about it. Determine what action is taken by the Department of Motor Vehicles and if that agency is even made aware of such violations.

EDUCATION AND TREATMENT

Drunk driver school (alcohol education) and treatment programs should come under thorough investigation for possible deficiencies.

Treatment programs often are not effective in keeping drunk drivers off the roads.

Alcohol education programs are a waste of time if poorly conducted, and can lead to additional violations by those who attend. Attempt to find answers to questions like these:

• Has the program been evaluated to determine its effect on drunk driving?

• Are repeat offenders sent through the same program again and again?

• What happens to an individual who shows up drunk, or to one who has been drinking prior to class?

• What happens when someone under court order to attend does not, or misses some sessions?

• If those in the program are obviously in need of treatment that is unavailable, are they sent back to the court for referral to an appropriate treatment center?

• Are separate programs available to meet the needs of young people?

• Are treatment and education programs regulated by the state?

A member of the task force might sit in on an education and a treatment program. And SADD members ought to be encouraged to attend teen programs. Qualified personnel from both programs should make a presentation to the task force.

SUGGESTION: Education and treatment is a complex area. Write or call the National Highway Traffic Safety Administration and the National Clearinghouse For Alcohol Information[1] for information. Also note that a panel of experts from the National Safety Council and the National Highway Traffic Safety Administration recently recommended that existing alcohol treatment programs not be used as **alternatives** to license suspension, revocation or other penalties. Such programs, they contend could better serve as an additional mandatory requirement for offenders.

DEPARTMENT OF MOTOR VEHICLES

Your state agency responsible for issuing driver licenses must also be on your list for a thorough check.

Determine if records are adequate and available. And what system is used when suspending or revoking the licenses of convicted drunk drivers.

Does the motor vehicle department have a poor computerized record-keeping system that does not provide timely information on past convictions to the courts?

Find out if convictions are promptly reported by the courts to the licensing agency and ascertain how long it takes before convictions are entered on a driver's record.

Learn what happens to out-of-state motorists convicted of drunk driving in your area. Is the record of conviction forwarded to the home state of the violator? If not, why not? And what about the other way around? An official from your department of motor vehicles should have the answers.

HOW TO INVESTIGATE
THE YOUTH PORTIONS OF THE
DRUNK-DRIVER CONTROL SYSTEM

Besides thoroughly examing the total system that deals with drunk drivers in your community, it is especially important to carefully inspect its "youth portions." It is a part of the system that needs special investigation for possible inadequacies.

If the youth subsystem is fine-tuned to the tolerances of available state-of-the-art technology, and kept that way, the death and injury rate for teen-agers will significantly and permanently decrease.

The subsystem includes the process of arrests involving teen-aged drunk drivers, through the final disposition of their cases and the environment surrounding the process. Every component of the youth part of the system must be thoroughly explored and documented so defects can be exposed and corrected. The investigation should be a part of the local task force process or a separate probe. Either way, it is important that it be accurate and complete and undertaken as soon as possible.

In addition to triggering an official investigation of the subsystem, the student group should conduct its own inquiry. This non-official study will serve as a double-check on the official probe and keep pressure on that group to do a good job.

The student survey may be undertaken by one individual or a team working together.

The major components of the youth subsystem include schools, police, prosecutors, courts, treatment and rehabilitation services, the state legislature and the governor, local government, the agency or commission responsible for alcohol beverage control and the motor vehicle licensing agency.

Here are some questions and approaches which might prove helpful in your investigation:

SCHOOLS

Determine what steps your school is undertaking to combat drunk driving. It could be that it is doing very little, or nothing. Each school needs a plan of action to curtail teen-involved alcohol crashes.

Did your school have a safe prom project or a safe ride

program last year? Why not? Are such programs planned for this year? Does the school actively encourage the use of safety belts and provide up-to-date course material on alcohol abuse and how it affects teen-agers? Does it offer a competent program to identify and refer drug abusers to appropriate treatment? (Remember: alcohol is a drug.) Are school administrators and teachers working with student and parent groups on the issue?

Trace your school's activities during the past several years that were supposed to help reduce the death and injury rate from alcohol-impaired driving. Are there any plans for the coming year? If none exist, complain to the Board of Education and your local news organizations. Every school needs such plans.

Complain loudly. It could be your life that is at stake.

POLICE

The police department should be exerting every effort to deter teen-agers from drinking and driving and let them know that if they do they will be apprehended and charged.

Also determine how many young people were arrested last year and if there are plans to increase the number.

Talk to officers who patrol the streets to learn how they handle teen-aged drunk drivers. If they suspect an individual of being too drunk to drive, do they notify his parents to avoid placing him in custody, or do they make a formal arrest? [2]

Are police encouraged or discouraged by their superiors to look for teen-aged drunk drivers? What happens after one is arrested?

Are police satisfied it is worth their time under the current system to arrest youngsters for this offense? Seek to determine what other problems police see in the system and what changes they recommend. Also check with officers who specialize in juvenile crime. Ask them what their problems are and get their recommendations for improvement. Are police enforcing alcohol beverage laws?

Are they preventing the sale of alcohol to minors and intoxicated persons? Are they using selective enforcement methods to control teen drinking drivers? Besides road-blocks, selective enforcement should include such tactics as targeting roads known for high drunk-driving activity and staking out parking lots of bars to catch such drivers before they endanger the public.

PROSECUTION

In some communities, juvenile drunk drivers are incor-rectly processed by prosecutors and their "crime" is not viewed as a very serious one. Such an attitude in a prosecutor's office can be deadly for innocent citizens and dangerous for teen-agers.

To find out what is going on in the prosecutor's office, ask questions. Learn exactly what takes place in the prosecution of a youth arrested for drunk driving. How long does it take for the case to go to trial? Is plea-bargaining going on? Do prosecutors do anything to stop the teen-ager from committing the same crime again?

COURTS

Investigate what happens to a teen-aged drunk driver in the courts. How is a first offender usually treated? What about a second or third offender? What happens to a teen-ager who violates probation rules? (Sometimes, nothing.)

What punishment and treatment options does the judge

have? Which ones are being used? How about pre-sentence investigations? Is an alcohol-abuse assessment obtained for each teen-ager?

Are those arrested for drunk driving treated as adults or as juveniles? Does the court notify the driver licensing agency? What happens to his license to drive? Is it suspended or revoked? Get a breakdown on how many went through the court system and what happened to them. What was the usual punishment?

TREATMENT AND REHABILITATION

In general, teen-agers who drink and drive are either abusing alcohol or simply do not care if they break the law and endanger themselves and the public. They may also stupidly drink too much and then ignorantly drive, oblivious to what can and often does happen. A teen-ager experimenting with alcohol who drives and is arrested, however, should be treated differently from a person who has a serious alcohol-abuse problem.

Just as it would be a waste of time and money to put a teen-ager, arrested for drunk driving after imbibing for the first time, in a resident treatment program for young alcoholics, it is also wrong to put a teen-age alcohol abuser in a simplistic education class and expect the problem to be corrected. Teen-agers have quite different needs. Some of their programs should stress alcohol education, while others focus on drug abuse treatment.

Are convicted teen-aged drunk drivers given the same alcohol education as adults? This is the wrong approach.

Court-ordered programs for teen-agers ought to be designed specifically for them. The programs should meet community or state minimum standards and be competently evaluated from time to time. Does such a program that is

137

properly evaluated exist in your community? If there is none, whatever does exist in your community may be a dangerous waste of time and money.

ALCOHOL BEVERAGE CONTROL

Alcohol beverage control is a part of the system that is often neglected or out of control. Merchants who sell beer, wine and liquor often do so illegally and get away with it. It's no secret that minors can buy beer and wine in most communities and that many bars routinely serve intoxicated or under-aged persons. And when a merchant is caught breaking the law, in many cases, very little ever happens to him.

Find out exactly what steps the agency charged with monitoring alcohol beverage laws in your community is taking to enforce the law.

What happens to a licensed establishment caught breaking the law? Usually, a minimal fine is the result. Ask why stiffer penalties are not meted out and why establishments that violate the law are not closed down more often. Publicize your findings. Such revelations can be a solid step toward achieving better enforcement and control of the laws governing the sale of intoxicants, especially to minors.

STATE DEPARTMENT OF MOTOR VEHICLES

When an individual of **any** age is convicted of driving while under the influence of alcohol or has refused to take a breath or other test, that information should be sent promptly to your Department of Motor Vehicles. In many cases, the agency does not receive such data.

Determine if such information is being forwarded to the

licensing agency in your state so appropriate action can be taken on drivers' license records. In some jurisdictions, court records involving teen-aged drunk drivers are not sent to the driver license agency. (This is a dangerous practice and must be corrected.) Find out what happens if the agency does get the information. Make sure you learn what actually is done, not what is prescribed by law. There can be a big difference. What is the agency planning to do about the problems it has?

THE REPORT

When your investigation of the "youth aspect" of the control system has been completed, a report should be drafted and made public. It should identify all problem areas, plus recommendations to correct them. The report should be presented to the task force and to the highest elected official in your community with a demand that he take quick action.

HOW TO FINANCE
NECESSARY DRUNK-DRIVER CONTROLS

It has been proven that it is possible to reduce deaths associated with alcohol-related crashes for short periods of time. But to lower the death rate permanently, it will be necessary to undertake and maintain costly additional efforts primarily at the local level of government.

Sufficient funds must be allotted to bring about an increase in arrests, better prosecution, pre-sentence alcohol-abuse assessments, efficient handling of drunk-driving cases by courts and judges, effective punishment and rehabilitation, a major publicity campaign and other needed efforts.

If funds are not forthcoming, drunk driving will remain largely uncontrolled and public safety will continue to be unnecessarily jeopardized. Any gains from massive citizen and media pressure will be short-lived and many people will continue to suffer in the future.

Money necessary for effective control is but a small fraction of the cost associated with the destruction of human life and property caused by drunk drivers. It is conservatively estimated that the alcohol-crash problem costs the nation more than $24 billion annually. (That's $24,000,000,000.00!) And that figure does not take into account the cost of human suffering, which cannot be calculated, or the loss to this country of the potential talents of those killed or disabled.

While better drunk-driver control programs will be expensive, the public need not pay one extra dime. The entire cost can and should be borne by the drunk drivers themselves through user fees and increased court costs, and by the alcohol beverage industry through earmarked taxes.

USER FEES AND COURT COSTS

In most states, fines, court costs and user fees assessed against convicted drunk drivers should be substantially increased and earmarked to help pay for effective control at the local level. SADD groups should evaluate the current fee system and demand changes in the law so fees generated by drunk-driving convictions can be returned to the community.

In New York, State Senator William T. Smith, whose daughter was killed by a drunk driver, worked for years without results to have effective legislation enacted. With citizen support, he finally achieved success.

Smith's efforts, with the support of the RID organization, produced a law that dramatically increased fines for drunk-driving convictions and set the stage for more comprehensive enforcement.

Under Smith's "STOP-DWI" legislation, first-time convictions were boosted from $50 to a new mandatory level of $250. Driving while intoxicated was raised to a $350 minimum mandatory fine with a $500 maximum. Subsequent convictions for both offenses carry correspondingly more severe penalties.

In addition, the STOP-DWI legislation provided new revenues to local governmental jurisdictions from the higher fines to apprehend and prosecute drunk drivers.

The New York law provides that fines collected trom drunk-driving convictions be returned to the counties for the creation of Special Traffic Option Programs for improved enforcement, prosecution, and adjudication efforts. To qualify for the funds, a jurisdiction must have a STOP-DWI coordinator who reports annually on program activities and how the money was spent to the county governing body and Department of Motor Vehicles.

THE NICKEL-A-DRINK TAX LAW

The nickel-a-drink tax concept is the brainchild of Forst Lowery, who was project director of the Hennepin County, Minnesota, Alcohol Safety Action Project. Several states are considering the proposal as a means of supporting a comprehensive alcohol safety program.

It calls for a five-cent tax to be levied against "on-sale" alcoholic beverages. The nickel-a-drink toll is an excise tax on the gross receipts from the sale of alcoholic beverages by wholesalers to retail dealers for the purpose of resale at an on-sale establishment by the glass or by the drink.

Beer, wine and distilled spirits would be subject to the tax. The Lowery proposal will make it possible to increase drunk-driving arrests and provide for **all** control costs, including rehabilitation and education. The cost to the consumer at a licensed established is about five cents per drink. The tax monies collected would be more than enough to pay for effective drunk-driver control. Surplus funds could be used for other alcohol-related problems in the community, such as child and spouse-abuse programs.

A nickel-a-drink tax, or an alternative measure to raise funds, should be enacted in every state. Student and citizen activist groups should have such bills introduced, then lobby to have them either enacted or placed on a state-wide referendum for the electorate to decide.

Lowery, who is a member of the Presidential Commission on Drunk Driving, says "It's time to get the drunk driver off the taxpayer's back." He has shown a way to do it. Complete literature on the nickel-a-drink law may be obtained by writing to: Forst Lowery, Alcohol Program Coordinator, Office of Traffic Safety: 207 Transportation Building, St. Paul, MN 55155. His phone number is (612) 296-9490.

NOTES

1. P.O. Box 2345, Rockville, Maryland 20852
2. If police are taking an "unarrest" option for teens suspected of driving impaired, this is a dangerous practice that should be halted immediately. By failing to arrest that particular teen-ager, they risk the danger that he or she will commit the offense again. This too often leads to tragedy.

8

HOW TO WORK WITH ELECTED OFFICIALS

Much of what must be done to bring the drunk-driving problem under control will take the cooperation and leadership of elected officials at all levels of government. However, even the most dedicated and concerned ones will accomplish little without public support. SADD groups must learn how to work with and support the efforts of those politicians who are sincerely endeavoring to solve the problem.

Working with a leader committed to doing his share means letting that official know your group supports his efforts and is willing and able to assist. Bring him up-to-date information on the problem and help him bring about corrective action.

Determine what plans he may have to attack the problem. If they are incomplete, explain strategies that have shown promise elsewhere and suggest that he use them. Show him this book.

If an office holder is serious about bringing the problem under control, the only method that will work is a competent, total systems approach. He must be aware of that crucial fact, and SADD groups should see to it that he is.

Many politicians, although they maintain they are in favor of getting drunk drivers off the roads, will barely lift a finger to do anything meaningful unless pressured by the voting public. That's the way the system usually works. Knowing this, SADD groups must not hesitate to bring such pressure to assure that the problem will be addressed with the vigor it deserves.

See that "reluctant" politicians get the message that drunk driving must be controlled. If people let this be known in no uncertain terms and protest loudly enough, authorities will respond. Galvanize your community into action to force elected officials to cooperate.

Working with politicians is an art that can be learned and used successfully by high school students. If you have discovered how to get along with your parents, teachers and school administrators, you can work with political leaders.

Remember that they depend on the goodwill of the public to remain in office. Working cooperatively with SADD buys a lot of good will for any politician. That translates into support for the next election, and they know it.

Most officials will, of course, say they are in favor of a group like SADD and its goals. But not all will mean it. You must distinguish between those who are sincere and those who are just opportunists.

When your group decides to push for specific reform legislation, ask legislators where they stand on the proposed law and what they will do to help get it enacted. Ask that you be kept informed, every step of the way, of the legislative process so that if the proposed law is stalled by committee tactics, SADD can initiate prompt action to force it out of committee. Have your state senator or delegate explain problems that might be encountered and what your group could do to help. The extent to which politicians cooperate and follow through with their promises to your SADD group are good indications of their sincerity.

If a state senator has agreed to introduce a bill that would immediately suspend the drivers' licenses of motorists who refuse to take an alcohol breath test (or fail it), your SADD unit should offer to participate in a press conference to help heighten public awareness for its need. Your group should also drum up citizen support for the bill.

Politicians can sometimes use an issue like drunk driving and the attendant publicity to further their careers, and are not above using a SADD group at a press conference to draw favorable media coverage. Some good will flow from such relationships, but do not expect this type politician to help bring the problem under control without continued and relentless pressure.

GETTING A BILL INTRODUCED

Having new state anti-drunk driving legislation introduced is easy. Getting it enacted into law is another matter.

After researching state laws that deal with the problem and identifying what changes or additional laws are needed, find one or more members of the legislature who will introduce the bills. Most will agree to do so, but it is best to have it done by a legislator who has a reputation for being effective and is a **heavyweight** in the General Assembly. If you work with a weak legislator, no matter how important and right the proposed bills are, the possibility of their passage is very slight. Select respected legislators of proven ability, rather than those who will latch on to your SADD group for selfish political purposes.

Ascertain the requirements to get a bill passed and signed by the governor in your state, then monitor it through each step. Have its sponsor keep your group posted of every twist and turn the measure takes in the legislative process. Many bills are referred to committee, where they often languish and die. But with the pressure generated by a citizen activist group, public hearings will be held and the bills can be forced out of committee. If a valid anti-drunk driving piece of legislation is stalled in committee, ask the chairman for an explanation. Pin him down for an answer. Confront him and his committee with your entire SADD group.

Put pressure on the chairman and members of the committee. Use the telephone tree concept (Chapter 4) to generate phone calls from constituents and, if necessary, conduct a demonstration at the state capitol. Get the governor and other prominent people to endorse the bill.

Keep in mind that in many states, strong anti-drunk driving proposals have been introduced in the legislatures year after year, only to be killed in lawyer-dominated committees. Some lawyer-legislators earn part of their living defending drunk drivers, and others would prefer not to offend special interest groups, such as bar owners. Such legislation fails because of public ignorance, the media's failure to cover the issue adequately, the indifference of politicians, and because there was no citizen pressure (coupled with effective lobbying) to force its passage. SADD and citizen activist groups **must** learn how to lobby. All backers of good causes find this out sooner or later.

HOW TO LOBBY FOR
BETTER DRUNK-DRIVING LAWS

There are a number of steps you can take to become an effective lobbyist. Many have been used successfully by victim activist groups to get tougher anti-drunk driving laws passed.

If these same steps are followed, they could lead to approval of reform drunk-driving legislation. But it takes work and commitment. SADD groups from several schools should share the task. A vigorous team lobbying effort by several SADD units cannot be beat. That is how powerful SADD can become when you learn how the system operates and how to influence it.

Try these approaches:

1. Evaluate exactly how the legislative process works in your state to understand how a bill becomes law. Call the governor's office and request a manual on the legislative process. Speak with legislative staff members and have them explain the system, as well as possible pitfalls that might be encountered.

2. Obtain copies of existing legislation in your state on drunk driving. Learn what the laws mean. If you have questions, seek answers from lawyers, prosecutors or judges. Be certain the person is qualified. Sometimes even judges do not understand all the laws they administer. If in doubt, get a second opinion.

3. Talk with other people who work in the drunk-driving system for their thoughts on what is wrong with existing laws and improvements needed.

4. Find out what model legislation has been proposed or adopted in other areas and compare them with your state laws. The National Safety Council has such information. Contact the NHTSA for a current list and brief explanation of suggested drunk-driving laws.[1]

5. Examine what you receive from NHTSA and note the laws your state does not have. Your group should consider supporting the passage of any or all of them. If

a new SADD unit is lobbying for the first time, it should pick one important bill and work on that. It is useless to "bite off more than you can chew." If several SADD groups work together, it is possible to lobby for a package of drunk-driving bills.

6. Investigate any new measures that were introduced, but failed to pass, in the previous three years. Obtain copies of the bills and the names of sponsors. Ask them and their staffs what roadblocks exist. Were the bills that were introduced any good? Determine who will be introducing such measures in the coming legislative session.

7. Locate a likely sponsor and ask that he or she introduce the legislation your SADD group has decided to support.

8. Generate publicity about the new bills. Schedule a press conference explaining the proposed legislation and issue news releases. Talk about the need for the bills whenever you are interviewed by the media.

9. Track the measures through every step of the legislative process. If necessary, contact the proper committee daily for information regarding their progress.

10. Make sure a hearing on the bills is scheduled in time to complete the other necessary steps required before they can become law. If no public hearing is set, demand that one be held and that you be notified by mail or phone so that members of your SADD group can attend. Let it be known there is widespread citizen and student support. Insist that your group be kept informed of everything that happens.

11. When the hearing dates are set, line up qualified students to testify before the committee. Also, have victims, police, judges, and experts testify on the

importance of the proposed anti-drunk driver legislation.

12. Have SADD members telephone or visit each committee member to educate them on the merits of the bills. Ask members how they intend to vote. **Get a commitment!** Let the legislators know that your group is building citizen pressure in favor of the proposed measures.

13. Exert the most severe pressure on the committee chairman. He has the power to get your bills out of committee. Do not believe him if he says otherwise. Does he have any objections to the bills? If they are unreasonable, put political pressure on the chairman. Criticize his actions in the media. Arrange a demonstration against him. Even consider burning him in effigy, if necessary.

    Let the public and the media know what is happening to your bills in the legislative process. Some of this may seem extreme, but we are dealing with a drastic problem. In any event, do not let your bills die in committee without a tremendous effort on your part to keep them alive.

14. Find other organizations that have lobbyists and ask them to help you persuade legislators that your bills are needed.

    Organize a meeting of lobbyists interested in drunk-driving legislation and plan a concerted attack. Insurance companies, medical societies and police all lobby for favorite bills. Many will help a student group, if requested.

15. Record how each committee member votes on the bills and keep the media informed. Let the legislators know you are doing this. It helps to hold their feet to the fire.

16. When the bills are before committee or the full house

or senate, have people call or write legislators and demand their support.

17. Educate all members of SADD regarding the bills and have them contact their local representatives to push for passage of the pending measures.

18. If there are several schools in your state, city or county with SADD organizations, arrange a joint meeting and divide the task of mounting citizen pressure. Generate mail from the public, influential citizens and organizations like the PTA to specific members of the legislature from their jurisdiction imploring them to vote in favor of the drunk-driving bills.

19. Determine which legislators are for or against the bills. Take a straw vote—ask each member, or at least your delegation, how they will vote. Concentrate on those opposed. Why are they against such legislation? There may be misinformation SADD can help straighten out.

20. Consider demonstrations, such as a candlelight vigil, at an appropriate time during the legislative process.

21. Write the editor of every newspaper in your state (use form letters if necessary) seeking support. Request editorials about the bills and the necessity to control drunk drivers.

22. Ask the governor to take a public position on the proposed legislation. If he will back the bills, request that he and his staff lobby for their passage. If the governor won't back the bills, find out why and if he does not have a good reason, mount a campaign against him.

Grass-roots lobbying is very effective, but it requires time and some trial and error to learn how to do it.

Although improved drunk-driving laws are desperately

needed in every state, it may take several years to get them. Lobbying by your SADD group this year should be continued the following session. Since some of your leaders will graduate next June, teach non-seniors the lobbying process so they may carry on the work. No matter what, do not give up. Remember the lives of many innocent people will depend on improved laws being passed.

A LEGISLATIVE PROJECT
ALL SADD GROUPS SHOULD CONSIDER

Many states still do not have a law that requires all children under age five to be in an approved child-restraint device whenever riding in an automobile. If your state does not have such a law (or the existing law is weak), spearhead a move to have a restraint law enacted or improved.

Why should a student group fighting drunk driving worry about a child-restraint law? The reason is that many small children killed or seriously injured in alcohol-related crashes could have been spared if they had been safely strapped in an approved child-restraint device. Despite their proven effectiveness, many parents still do not use them.

It is estimated that only one out of ten children under the age of five is put into a child-restraint device. And many parents who do use them, do so incorrectly.

Young children do not possess the ability to make the life and death decision as to whether or not to use a restraint device. Parents who do not use restraint seats are neglecting their child's right to safety. If a collision occurs, the failure to use a restraint device is akin to child abuse.

Does your state have an effective child-restraint law? Call or write the National Safety Council and the National Highway Traffic Safety Administration for information on child-restraint devices and copies of model legislation.

If your state has no child-restraint law, find out if one has been introduced in the past two years. If so, locate the sponsor and find out why the measure failed.

Follow the lobbying instructions in this chapter and develop a plan for a child-restraint bill in your state. With dedication, SADD can lead the way to the enactment of a good child-restraint law. It will save lives. Working on such a law is also good training for your efforts on behalf of drunk-driving legislation. If your state has a child-restraint law, check to see if it is being enforced and if it is an "effective" law versus a law that is full of loopholes. If the existing law is weak, work for improvements.

VOTING RECORDS

Your SADD unit should monitor the voting records of all elected officials from your jurisdiction on drunk-driving bills at all stages of the legislative process.

These records should be made available to the media and compiled in a SADD newsletter to be sent to each student's home so voting parents will be aware of legislators who are not acting responsibly. Observing politicians closely will usually ensure that they do the right thing.

ELECTIONS

When an election is held in your area, learn where candidates stand on drunk driving. If they have a bad record on the issue, or will not pledge to work actively for passage of needed legislation, oppose their candidacy.

All seekers of major office in your jurisdiction should be asked specific questions concerning their position on drunk driving and what they intend to do about it if elected.

Prepare an issue paper on their positions. Distribute it to the parents of all students at your school and recommend that they refuse to vote for anyone unwilling to work for drunk-driving reform.

Your SADD organization should make drunk driving an election issue, because in its purest sense, drunk driving is a political problem. Without the honest support of elected officials, the problem will never be resolved. Another effective move to convince politicians to support your cause is to campaign only for candidates who favor drunk-driver reform. Volunteer to work for such candidates.

Many elections for senate and house seats are won by very small vote margins. Every vote counts.

If they work hard enough, SADD members can prevent an errant politician from being elected. And the fear that such groups have become politically influential and can possibly alter the outcome of an election will help keep other politicians in line.

It is unfortunate, but true, that people often vote stupidly. Many simply will not take the time to become familiar with either issues or candidates. Too often, people vote for someone because they like the way he looks or the sound of his name. That's one major reason why our legislative process can let a serious problem like drunk driving slip through the cracks. At the very least, your SADD group can inform the public of a candidate's position.

Another problem is that many who could vote are too lazy or indifferent to even register. SADD groups must help get out the vote. If parents express concern about drunk driving and promise to help bring the problem under control, convince them to register and vote for candidates genuinely supporting the drunk-driving cause.

In later years, when there are SADD groups in the majority of communities, there will be the need to hold an annual statewide meeting to plot a course of legislative action and share the work to be done. When that day comes, rapid progress will follow and SADD will have become a powerful political force that cannot be ignored.

CONGRESS

SADD members should write or visit their members of Congress and ask what they have done or plan to do about drunk driving. Tell them you intend to report back to your student body and their parents. This should ensure that your request won't be treated lightly and will evoke a proper response. You have every right to know what is going on in Washington, but you must be assertive.

Let your congressmen and senators know you expect the federal government to do all in its power to help your state and community win the battle against drunk drivers. Suggest that money be appropriated to help fund efforts at the state and local levels. No matter what they tell you, Congress can find money for whatever project it favors.

Federal funds are wasted every year on questionable projects with a much lower moral priority than drunk driving. Ask lawmakers why the alcohol beverage tax has not been raised in 30 years and what they plan to do about it. It's a fair question. And it deserves to be answered.

THE PRESIDENTIAL COMMISSION
ON DRUNK DRIVING

The idea for a Presidential Commission on Drunk Driving originated in the news room of WDVM-TV in Washington following a news series in May 1980 about Laura Lamb and the lax laws in Maryland that allowed such a tragedy to happen. The concept for the Commission was the brainchild of the author of this book.

In an attempt to get the President to appoint such a Commission, this writer tried a number of strategies, including in 1980 (during the Carter administration) organizing a White House picket demonstration of victims, and a Capitol Hill press conference.

While executive director of MADD, this writer drafted a petition and launched a nationwide petition drive calling for the establishment of the Commission. Although these moves helped to publicize the issue, the request for the Commission was ignored. After leaving MADD over a dispute about policy, I made a presentation in 1981 to the annual Board of Directors meeting of the American Council on Alcohol Problems (ACAP). I drafted a letter to President Reagan calling for the establishment of the Commission and it was signed by 45 executives of state, national and international organizations and religious groups attending the meeting.

That letter was ignored by the White House. The same letter, with minor changes, was later taken to Congress and as a result of the leadership of William Plymat, executive director of ACAP, and the efforts of the members of his organization, a majority of Congress was convinced to sign it. Other organizations including RID, Maryland MADD, the National Association of Evangelicals and many others also worked to help get the Commission established.

This historic letter was hand-delivered to the President by Congressman Jim Hansen of Utah who had been a victim of two drunk-driving collisions.

This time the White House could not ignore the issue and the President agreed to establish the Commission.

ACAP has not gotten the recognition it deserves for the creation of the Commission; as usual, others have rushed in to ride the coattails of this issue after much of the difficult work had been done.

155

THE WHITE HOUSE

Despite the appointment of the Presidential Commission on Drunk Driving and other federal activities that resulted from citizen protests, President Reagan, as this is written, has been dangerously negligent in the way he has handled the issue.

When initial requests were made for the President to establish a Commission on Drunk Driving, top White House aides told this writer the White House did not want to take on the drunk-driving issue because they said it would interfere with a planned war on illegal drugs. This, despite the fact that alcohol abuse and alcohol-related crashes take a much higher toll of teen-agers and people of all ages than illegal drugs. The aides failed to give the drunk-driving issue the attention it deserved.

Had President Reagan received competent advice on what he could do to combat drunk driving and acted promptly, it is probable that thousands who were subsequently killed and tens of thousands seriously injured in alcohol-related crashes might not have been.

Put another way, President Reagan, for whatever reason, did not take available steps that would have significantly reduced death and injury in every state in the nation. As a consequence, the horrible toll of deaths and injuries from drunk driving continued.

What should the President have done?

For starters, President Reagan should have taken the time to look more fully into the drunk-driving issue and its impact on the American public, then ordered a highly-skilled team of experts to put together a valid plan of attack using state-of-the-art knowledge in an all-out effort to reduce death and injury at the state and local levels.

Following this, the President could have used the power

of his office to go on prime-time television and tell the American people the real magnitude of the drunk-driving crisis. He could then have outlined plans to combat the problem. For example, President Reagan could have let the public know the importance of competent task forces at each local level of government and ordered the Department of Transportation to prepare information packets to clearly explain what should be done and how to do it. He could have encouraged the formation of SADD and activist groups in every community in the country and ordered the federal government to assist in establishing such programs. He could have suggested that every school in the nation have a "Project Graduation."

Had the President done these things, it is reasonable to assume that concerned citizens throughout the United States would have demanded such efforts be undertaken. There would have been enormous progress by now in many states and communities. Numerous lives would have been saved.

Through key advisers, the President was asked several times to alert the public to the problem and tell the nation what should be done. A specific plan of attack designed to significantly reduce the death toll was presented to John Volpe, chairman of the President's Commission, but the report was ignored and nothing of substance happened. The same plan was also transmitted to the President by Senator John Danforth of Missouri, but it was still ignored.

Did the President fail to perform his duty and protect public safety? What do you think?

Why has the President failed to act? Perhaps it is because his staff has not advised him correctly. Perhaps it is because the alcohol beverage industry, which has White House ties, is fearful of what will happen to their profits if the country declares war on drunk driving and then fights to win. There is no question that their profits would go down. It is a small price that the beverage alcohol industry is unwilling to pay for substantially less human suffering.

If a relative or friend recently suffered death or injury at the hands of a drunk driver, President Reagan must share much of the blame. He failed to act in the best interest of the public.

The President's Commission on Drunk Driving has made some positive suggestions in its interim report, but because of the way the Commission was controlled by the Reagan Administration, it predictably fell far short of what is needed. "Public hearings" held by the Commission were not open to public input. The choice of witnesses was not unbiased.

What can SADD do about this regrettable and negligent Presidential failure? Plenty!

Fortunately, we live in America. We have freedom of speech. And we have the right to participate in how we are governed. What each SADD group must do is undertake a presidential letter-writing campaign to protest his inactivity.

Ask all members of your student body to take home a copy of the following letter and sign it, along with their parents, and mail it to the President. Eventually, if enough letters pour into the White House, he may rethink his position and take responsible action. The President claims to be concerned about the drunk-driving problem. **Make him prove it.**

LETTER TO THE PRESIDENT

President Ronald Reagan
The White House
Washington D.C. 20500

Dear Mr. President,

As you know, drunk driving is a very serious problem in every state and community in the nation. Our lives are in danger because our streets are not safe from drunk drivers. We are very concerned about this.

Drunk driving has become the most frequently committed violent crime in our nation and is one of the the most serious domestic health and safety threats Americans face every day of their lives.

We feel you have not shown effective leadership to help bring this nightmarish problem under control.

We ask that you declare war on drunk drivers and order the efforts necessary to win. With your leadership we could substantially reduce alcohol-related death and injury throughout the country.

There is no excuse for your continued refusal to attack this problem in a meaningful way. Please do what is right and best for us all. You have a moral obligation to do so. We will accept no less from our President.

Sincerely,

If enough SADD groups take part in this project, it is extremely unlikely that President Reagan will ignore the request. If he does, ask your parents not to vote for him if he runs for office again.

Besides taking copies of the presidential protest letter home, students should also circulate it to other concerned groups. SADD should issue a press release to all newspapers, television and radio stations noting that they are participating in a nationwide effort to force the President to do a better job of protecting the public from drunk drivers.

THE NATIONAL HIGHWAY TRAFFIC SAFETY ADMINISTRATION

The National Highway Traffic Safety Administration (NHTSA) is the federal agency created by Congress to deal with such issues as drunk driving. Many NHTSA staffers are dedicated career employees who have been working for years to combat drunk driving. But there is a problem at the NHTSA. It is operated by political appointees who in many cases have no expertise whatever in the highway safety field. They make life and death decisions based on political considerations, rather than facts. The career staffers bend with the political winds. The public suffers as a result.

The NHTSA administration is supposed to be a safety agency concerned with doing what is necessary to protect the public.

There should be no room for politics in such a vital agency.

As presently operated, NHTSA is failing to do its job properly and protect the public.

One example is drunk driving. In the decade prior to 1980, NHTSA had spent more than $100 million on the issue, with little, if any, result. Then in 1980, the agency had to be pushed into action by news reports of the mounting tragedy and by outraged citizens.

During the decade when the money was spent, an estimated 250,000 died in alcohol-related crashes. By 1980, the problem was projected to get worse. Yet knowledge existed that could have prevented what many now call "America's greatest tragedy." It should not have been allowed to happen. The NHTSA is largely to blame.

The agency failed its mission. There is no excuse for the fact that in 1983, drunk driving is still the leading cause of death of young people in this country.

Another problem that should be mentioned is the manner in which the agency handles its contracting. Tax dollars that should be spent to protect the public are being wasted. That waste cost large numbers of people their lives.

The Congress, which has oversight responsibilities for the agency, should order a full-scale General Accounting Office (GAO) investigation of NHTSA contracting procedures. In fact, it is my belief that a complete probe of the entire agency is in order.

NOTES

1. This is not to suggest that all proposed state laws which are federally endorsed should be supported in your state. Each law recommended by the federal government should be carefully considered and background information on how it is working in other states obtained.

CONCLUSION

There should by now be no question in your mind that drunk driving is the scourge of every state and community in the country, and that everybody should be deeply concerned. But unless more people become involved in reform efforts, many will meet tragic death or serious injury every day on our streets, roads and highways.

It is a problem that you, personally, must do something about, because the bitter truth is that today or any day, without warning, you could become a victim.

You also should have learned from this book that public officials in your area most likely have not and are not doing what they should to protect you and your family. Drunk driving is not a technical problem. In its most meaningful sense, it is a political problem that can be attacked through organized grass-roots pressure.

But this book's most important message is to warn you that your life is in danger because drunk driving is rampantly out of control. If you fail to take immediate steps to help solve the problem, you may pay a fearful price.

We have sought to provide useful, practical information to help save lives and prevent injuries. Now that you have this knowledge, you have some choices to make. You may totally ignore the situation and hope that you will not be the one person out of two whom NHTSA predicts will be involved in an alcohol-related crash in his lifetime. Or that

162

if you are, you will not be killed or physically impaired for the rest of your life. These are shortsighted choices, because sooner or later drunk driving is going to bring heartache into your life. The odds are stacked against you.

Other options are to develop the habit of always wearing safety belts and never, under any circumstances, riding with anyone who has been drinking excessively. If you care anything at all about your life, you should at least make these two choices.

You should also consider supporting the work of citizen and student activist groups or helping organize such a unit in your school or community. Unless organized student and citizen power is unleashed, large numbers of innocent people will continue to perish or face serious injuries in alcohol-related crashes. That is because, in general, elected and appointed officials simply will not take the necessary steps to alleviate the situation until they receive a public mandate forcing them to do so.

Before you make what could be one of the more important decisions of your life, heed this message from Tom Sexton, co-leader of the Maryland chapter of MADD, whose 15-year-old son was killed by a drunk driver. Until then, Tom and his wife, Dot, were unaware of the terrible threat drunk drivers pose for everyone. But now they have learned a great deal about the problem, including the fact that many lives can be saved if enough people get involved. That's the message they have for you. When asked what he would most recommend to the youth of our nation, their parents and teachers, Tom Sexton's reply was short but to the point: "Get involved."

"The strategies and suggestions in this book," he said, and I agree, "are only words on paper. Unless put into action, nothing will happen. Take these words and put them into action...**GET INVOLVED!**"

APPENDICES

1. Recommended Drunk-Driving Laws

Not one state in the nation has all the drunk-driving laws necessary to provide maximum protection.

One of the best sources of information on drunk-driving legislative matters is the National Safety Council (NSC). In early 1983, according to the NSC, at least 40 states had drunk-driving legislation pending and 30 states were considering child-restraint laws. The NSC has a *Policy Update* available at no cost that outlines the status of drunk-driving and child-restraint legislation on a state-by-state basis as well as other news of interest. Write to the NSC and ask for a copy of their latest legislative *Policy Update* and to be placed on their mailing list. The address is: Chuck Hurley, Executive Director, Office of Federal Affairs, 1705 De-Sales Street, N.W., Washington, D.C. 20036.

The following list of drunk-driving laws are just some of those needed in states that have not already enacted them.

Raising the Drinking Age to 21—Young people and people who make their living selling alcoholic beverages may think this law is unfair. Maybe it is, but it saves young lives. According to the Presidential Commission on Drunk Driving, "There is a direct correlation between the minimum drinking age and alcohol-related crashes...Studies have shown that raising the legal drinking age produced an average annual reduction of 28 percent in nighttime fatal crashes involving 18- to 21-year old drivers. In order to reduce the death rate of American youth, the minimum drinking age for all alcoholic beverages should be raised to 21."

Dram Shop Law—Any person selling or serving alcoholic beverages to an intoxicated person or a minor who kills or injures an innocent person should be held liable for civil negligence (as well as criminal negligence). A Dram shop law makes those responsible pay for their negligence. Sellers of alcoholic beverages oppose these types of laws for obvious reasons. Their opposition should be ignored. They have no right to act negligently. If they do, they ought to pay for the damages they cause. Dram shop laws

164

facilitate compensation to innocent victims and help deter illegal sales.

Prohibition of Alcohol Beverage Consumption in Motor Vehicles—It's just plain wrong to allow people to drink while driving. Yet many states and local communities do just that. There should be a law to prohibit the possession of an open alcoholic beverage container in the passenger compartment of a motor vehicle. It's just common sense.

Plea-Bargaining—This common practice should be banned by law in every state. The Presidential Commission on Drunk Driving correctly recommends that "Prosecutors should charge accurately, not overcharge or undercharge, and insist upon conviction on the appropriate charge. Prosecutors should not routinely plea-bargain driving-under-the-influence charges to non alcohol-related offenses. Plea-bargaining undermines the express will of the electorate and minimizes the consequence of engaging in illegal behavior. No driving-under-the-influence charge should be reduced or dismissed unless a written declaration is filed by the prosecutor stating why the interest of justice uniquely requires a reduction or why the charge cannot be proven beyond a reasonable doubt." Lawyers who make their living defending drunk drivers will oppose this type of law. It gives them no room to maneuver for their clients. Their opposition should be ignored and the public interest put first.

Preliminary Breath Testing—The standard field sobriety test (walking a straight line, picking up coins from the ground, etc.) used in most states is not accurate. An experienced drinker can learn how to fool it. Police need a law that will allow them to use a preliminary breath test device (PBT) which is accurate.

Adequate Funding for Control Measures—Laws must be enacted in each state that will provide sufficient funds to pay for all steps necessary to protect the public from drunk drivers. Sources for these funds include increasing taxes on alcoholic beverages, ABC license fees, and offender fines and fees. Congress should also increase the federal excise tax on alcohol. The alcohol beverage industry does not want their taxes raised. Their wishes should be ignored. It's time they paid their fair share to control a problem they help cause.

Administrative Revocation Law—Iowa enacted a tough drunk-driving law that gives law enforcement authorities the power to immediately suspend a driver's license if a person is found to have .10 percent or more alcohol in their blood. In the first 3 months the law was in effect, the number of alcohol-related fatalities was cut in half, according to William Plymat, Executive Director of the American Council on Alcohol Problems (ACAP) and a member of the Presidential Commission on Drunk Driving. This type of law is desperately needed in every state, but keep in mind that new laws alone will not work for the long run. A total systems approach is needed. An 18-minute video tape program on administrative revocation in Iowa is available from ACAP for a nominal charge. Write for information. ACAP, 2908 Patricia Drive, Des Moines, Iowa 50322. Or call (515) 255-4430

.08 Presumptive Level of Under the Influence—According to the Presidential Commission, "Medical and driving demonstration studies show that most people are under the influence at a blood alcohol level of .08 percent. State law should recognize this fact and presume that people are under the influence at this level and lack the ability to safely drive. Two states (Idaho and Utah) have such laws."

.10 Illegal Per Se Law—Individuals with a blood alcohol content of .10 percent or higher are under the influence and lack the ability to drive safely. Laws making it illegal to drive with these levels of alcohol content in the blood increase the certainty of conviction, reduce litigation time and costs, and enhance public safety," according to the interim report of the Presidential Commission on Drunk Driving. "Twenty-three states have adopted this 'illegal per se law.' A person should be deemed to be in violation of this 'illegal per se law' if the blood alcohol test was taken within three hours of arrest and showed .10 percent or higher."

Child-Restraint Law—This law provides lifesaving protection to young children. There is **not one** valid reason for any state in the nation to continue to refuse to enact this type of law.

Victim Impact Statements—A law in each state should be enacted to require courts to establish procedures giving a victim or the victim's family the right to state their views prior to sentencing in cases where serious injury or death results from an alcohol-related crash.

Mandatory 48 Hours in Jail—This type of law is doomed to failure and should be opposed. It is probably the worst type of law a state can enact. There are not enough jail cells, and judges will not routinely sentence people to jail for a first offense of drunk driving. Stiff fines, alcohol-abuse assessments coupled with proper education and treatment, loss of license and perhaps community service are much harsher penalties and will be more effective than sentencing people to two days in jail for a first offense. If a person is an alcoholic or has a drug abuse problem with alcohol, putting him or her in jail for two days in most cases simply will not do any good. The Presidential Commission recommends 48 hours in jail for first offenders. Its position on this matter is not well thought-out and should be ignored.

Bankruptcy—Under current federal bankruptcy laws, a drunk driver can kill or seriously injure an innocent person and to escape civil liability can file for bankruptcy. Driving drunk is an intentional act and is a crime. To let a drunk driver escape his or her responsibility to his or her victim is outrageous and unjust. This loophole in the law must be corrected by Congress.

2. The Term "Drunk Driver"

The term "drunk driver" as used in this book refers to any person who drinks alcoholic beverages (beer, wine, or distilled spirits) and then drives while impaired. In the majority of states it is illegal to drive with a blood alcohol concentration (BAC) of .10 percent or above.

To reach .10 percent BAC, the average-size adult male weighing 140 pounds would need to consume four, ounce and a half drinks or four, 12 ounce beers within an hour. A person with a BAC of .10 is too impaired to drive safely. However, impairment can occur at a much lower BAC. While the majority of states set the legal limit at .10 percent BAC, it is important to note that the majority of the rest of the civilized world sets the legal limit at half that rate, or .05 percent.

It is also important to understand that there is no stereotypical "drunk driver." A drunk driver can be young or old, male or female, rich or poor, a light social drinker or an alcoholic. Anyone can be a drunk driver, even those who believe they do not drink to excess.

According to the Alcohol Research Information Service,[1] beginning with the first drink, alcohol starts to slow down reaction time, impair judgement and cut down overall driving skills. One of the first effects of alcohol is to increase a person's self-confidence at the same time it decreases a person's driving skills.

Even though the legal limit for drunk driving in most states is .10 percent BAC, driving skills are reduced long before that much alcohol is in the body. In other words, it is possible to be "legally" not under the influence of alcohol, but actually "drunk" enough to cause an alcohol-related crash.

For example, a driver is twice as likely to cause a collision with only a .06 percent BAC as is a completely sober driver. (A 110-pound person could reach a BAC level of .06 percent with two drinks in a half-hour period.)

Long before most people are aware, long before there are any obvious signs of drunkenness, alcohol will reduce the driver's tolerance to glare, cut down peripheral (side) vision, cause the driver to underestimate speed and distance, and encourage impulsive response and risk-taking.

Studies have shown that younger, less experienced drivers are affected adversely by smaller amounts of alcohol than older, more experienced drivers. Studies have also shown that beer drinkers are just as likely to get involved in drunk-driving crashes as are drinkers who have had wine or liquor.

While anyone who drinks can become a "drunk driver" it is also important to recognize that alcohol abusers are responsible for a significant share of the tragedy that results from alcohol-related crashes.

According to federal data, the average BAC of drinking drivers involved in fatal crashes is .20 percent, double the legal limit. This means that the average driver who kills or is killed on the highway has had about 15 drinks before getting behind the wheel. And the NHTSA claims that there is strong evidence that most alcohol-related fatal crashes are caused not by the many social drinkers, but by the relatively few heavy or problem drinkers. (This statement should not be taken to mean that just getting problem drinkers off the road will solve the problem. Social drinkers also kill and maim, and they too must be removed from our roads.) Drivers with a BAC of .15 percent are 25 times as likely to cause a fatal crash as a driver who had not been drinking.

SUGGESTION: To gain appreciation for the effects of alcohol on a person's driving skills and understanding of BACs and their relationship to driving, obtain a free copy of the movie *Under the Influence* from the NHTSA. The movie could be shown at SADD and task force meetings.

Notes:

1. Alcohol Research Information Service, 1120 East Oakland Avenue, Lansing, Michigan 48906.

3. Press Release for a Press Conference

August 25, 1980
PRESS CONFFRENCE
For further information
Contact Sandy Golden at
916-966-0000

M.A.D.D. MOTHERS AGAINST DRUNK DRIVERS
PRESS CONFERENCE

A press conference on the state-wide drunk-driving problem in California will be held on Tuesday, August 26, 1980 at 10:30 A.M. in the Governor's Press Room on the first floor of the state Capitol Building by the president of M.A.D.D., Candy Lightner.

At that time Candy Lightner, whose 13-year-old daughter was killed earlier this year by a repeat offender drunk driver, will announce a state-wide petition drive aimed at getting drunk drivers off the road and will publicly ask Governor Brown to appoint a task force charged with the responsibility of developing solutions to the state's drunk-driving problem.

The Identical twin of the slain girl will talk briefly on the issue and the principal of Del Campo High School, Eleanor Brown, will also speak out.

Starting at 10 A.M. on Tuesday a demonstration in support of the task force and reform of the drunk-driving problem will take place at the North entrance of the Capitol Building. About 20 high school students will picket and gather signatures on the petition.

Drunk driving is the number one highway traffic safety problem in California. Over 2,500 people were killed in alcohol-related crashes in 1979 and more than 73,000 were injured.

4. Petition Used to Obtain a State Task Force

M.A.D.D. MOTHERS AGAINST DRUNK DRIVING

To the Honorable Jerry Brown,
Drunk Driving is the number one highway traffic safety problem in the state of California by a very wide margin.

A significant number of California citizens who innocently come into contact with drunk drivers are unnecessarily losing their lives or are being seriously injured—many crippled or impaired for life.

According to the California Highway Patrol, over 2,500 people were killed during 1979 in alcohol-related crashes and over 73,000 people were injured.

The drunk-driving problem is not and has not been adequately or effectively addressed by the state.

And as a result, the life of every California citizen is threatened or affected by drunk drivers—every day.

Therefore: We the undersigned call on Governor Brown to take a firm and public leadership role and use the full powers of his office to address and where possible to correct the drunk-driving problem in the state of California.

Specifically we ask that the Governor appoint a task force, not to study the problem because it has been studied enough, but to develop realistic solutions to the problem which can be advocated and implemented by the Governor.

We ask that the task force be adequately funded and staffed and that the task force be required to issue a public report by January 1, 1981. We also ask that the Governor, through his office, help seek national reform of the drunk-driving problem.

Respectfully signed:

NAME	ADDRESS	PHONE

When completed, please return to: Mothers Against Drunk Drivers, P.O. Box H-C, Fair Oaks, Ca 95628, (916) 966-0000.

5. Letter Used to Obtain a Local Task Force

Maryland Chapter of MADD
3113 Tinder Place
Bowie, Maryland 20715

Mr. Lawrence J. Hogan, Sr.
Prince George's County Executive

Dear Mr. Hogan:
We are Tom and Dot Sexton. Our 15-year-old son Tommie was killed by a drunk driver on July 12, 1980. Since that date we have been working very hard at making our state legislators as well as our fellow citizens aware of the carnage on Maryland highways.
Drunk driving is one of the least understood yet most serious health hazards. Drunk driving is a national, state and local problem. Significant reduction of the human suffering caused by drunk drivers can be achieved at the county level. A solution-oriented task force is an effective beginning.
We would like to meet with you and discuss the possibility of forming a solution-oriented task force on the drunk-driving problem in Prince George's County. The task force should take a total systems approach to the problem and develop any and all possible solutions that will lead to a reduction of death and injury caused by drunk drivers.
MADD has recently organized in the county and has been developing broad-based community support for reform of the drunk-driving problem. MADD will shortly call for similar task forces in Montgomery and Frederick Counties. It is my sincere hope that Prince George's County will become a model for the rest of the state and nation to follow when it comes to abating drunk driving.
The victims of drunk drivers and many concerned citizens will not rest until everything possible is being done to combat the problem. We look forward to your cooperation and support.

Sincerely,

Tom and Dot Sexton
MADD-Coordinators
Prince George's County

171

6. Letter Endorsing Local Task Forces

January 22, 1982

National Safety Council

Mr. John Herrity
Chairman, Fairfax Board
   of Supervisors
4100 Chainbridge Rd.
Fairfax, VA

Dear Mr. Herrity:

The drunk driving problem is probably the most difficult
public health issue facing the country today. More than
26,000 Americans are expected to die this year on our
nation's highways from alcohol-related motor vehicle
crashes. In addition, roughly 650,000 Americans will suffer disabling injuries. Even more tragic, a dispropor-
tionate number of those victims are young people, under
the age of 25 for whom alcohol-related crashes are the
leading cause of death.

For these reasons, the National Safety Council strongly
supports the formation of local task forces to combat
this problem. Through these local efforts it is possible
to identify the problems and solutions specific to the
community's individual needs.

By establishing a task force, Fairfax County can take
a lead role in this campaign to curb the senseless
slaughter and thus become a part of the solution to
the problem.

Good luck on your efforts.

                              Sincerely,

                              Charles A. Hurley
                              Executive Director
                              Federal Affairs

CAH: nb

1705 De Sales Street N.W.   A Nongovernmental
Washington, D.C. 20036   Not for profit
202-293-2270   Public Service Organization

7. Court Monitoring Letter

RID – USA

HEADQUARTERS

A CITIZENS' PROJECT TO REMOVE INTOXICATED DRIVERS

Dear Judge

This letter introduces you to RID-CD, the Capital District chapter of RID-NYS, a citizen group organized to Remove the Intoxicated Driver in New York State. As some of our members plan to visit your court from time to time, you might like to know more about our organization.

We have several objectives:

1) To educate ourselves and the public about the ways that our present laws and regulations work, or fail, to protect the public from death and injury due to drunken drivers.

2) To raise the consciousness of public officials – judges, officers, prosecutors, and administrators – regarding their duties and opportunities to deal responsibly and constructively with this urgent public safety problem.

3) Aid the victims of drunken driving and their families.

4) Encourage the development and lobby for passage of more effective laws dealing with the alcoholic driver.

It is very important that drivers charged with DWI are NOT ALLOWED to satisfy such charges by pleading to anything other than DWI or DWAI. Fines for reckless driving or other substitute charges only mask the problem, invite continuing abuse, and often lead later, to death or permanent injuries. Sentencing, in some cases, undoubtedly presents judges with a tough decision, particularly where a breadwinner's job may be at stake. We believe courts should make more use of weekend jail sentencing. Where there has been a serious accident, courts should use their option under the law, to summarily lift a driver's license when arraigned and while awaiting trial. Driving is a privelege, not a right. Courts must protect the public's right to safe streets and highways.

In dealing with DWI cases, we hope that the atmosphere of the court will be as serious as the problem merits. Proceedings should not only be open, but audible to the public, so the defendant's name, the charges and the disposition are clear.

Our members look forward to observing your court and to meeting you. Your experience as a judge has probably given you further insights into this difficult area. We will be glad to receive your opinion regarding what laws or procedures might help to reduce the present heavy toll on our streets and highways.

Sincerely,

Doris Aiken

Doris Aiken
President

P.O. Box 520, Schenectady, N.Y. 12301

8. News Story on a New SADD Group

SADD to petition governor

By Mark Foster

A group of St. Charles High School students will gather signatures Wednesday on a petition asking Governor James Thompson to establish a state task force to fight drunken driving.

The petition is an effort by the newly formed Students Against Drunken Driving, which claims 78 members, to reduce alcohol-related driving accidents and fatalities.

The petition asks that a state task force investigate current drunken driving controls, and recommend improvements to further reduce drunken driving problems.

Once the petition drive is completed, the students hope to make an appointment with Thompson so that they can present the petition to him personally, said Norman Widerstrom, high school dean.

The purpose of SADD has been to "heighten concern and awareness of the issue, so that people will think twice before they drink and drive," said Garrick Veidel, one of the student organizers.

Brigitte Sames, another of the student organizers, added SADD's future plans include setting up a hotline where persons who have been drinking can call for a ride.

However, most of the efforts of the organization will be to make drunken driving "a social stigma," said Widerstrom, emphasizing the educational role of the school.

One of the speakers to address St. Charles students this year was Sandy Golden, a Maryland man who left his career as a journalist to work on the drunken driving issue, which he had been investigating as a reporter, according to Widerstrom.

It was Golden's talk that got her involved in SADD, said Sames, adding that the "frightening" reality of drunken driving statistics were another factor.

Widerstrom organized SADD through a $1,489 state grant.

The organization is the first in Illinois, he said, and is also unique because Kane County has been designated as the pilot county for the development for a comprehensive approach to the drunken driving problem.

Law enforcement, the state's attorney, courts and schools need to work together, Widerstrom said.

Police and the courts need to "tighten up" enforcement and penalties against drunk drivers, added Sames.

Wednesday's petition sign up will be preceded by a SADD sponsored talk from Kane County Coroner Mary Lou Kearns on Tuesday.

Another such program in May will include representatives from Mothers Against Drunken Driving.

(Reprinted with permission from the **St. CHARLES CHRONICLE**
Friday, March 4, 1983)

INDEX

Index